Charles Busch

About the Author

DR. LAURA SCHLESSINGER holds a postdoctoral certification and licensing in Marriage and Family Therapy from the University of Southern California, and a license in Marriage, Family and Child Counseling from the State of California. She is the author of seven *New York Times* bestsellers as well as four children's books. She is also the host of an internationally syndicated radio program and is an avid sailor, bicyclist, power walker, and weight lifter. Dr. Laura raises money for Operation Family Fund, which supports families of fallen soldiers, by selling her handcrafted jewelry. Dr. Laura lives in Southern California with her husband.

The Proper Care and Feeding of Husbands

Dr. Laura C. Schlessinger

HARPER

NEW YORK • LONDON • TORONTO • SYDNEY

HARPER

A hardcover edition of this book was published in 2004 by HarperCollins
Publishers.

THE PROPER CARE AND FEEDING OF HUSBANDS. Copyright © 2004 by Dr. Laura C.
Schlessinger. All rights reserved. Printed in the United States of America. No
part of this book may be used or reproduced in any manner whatsoever without written permission except in the case of brief quotations embodied in critical articles and reviews. For information address HarperCollins Publishers, 10
East 53rd Street, New York, NY 10022.

HarperCollins books may be purchased for educational, business, or sales pro-
motional use. For information please write: Special Markets Department,
HarperCollins Publishers, 10 East 53rd Street, New York, NY 10022.

FIRST HARPER PAPERBACK PUBLISHED 2006.

The Library of Congress has catalogued the hardcover edition as follows:
Schlessinger, Laura.
    The proper care and feeding of husbands / Laura Schlessinger.
        p.   cm.
    ISBN 0-06-052061-2
    1. Marriage. 2. Husbands—Psychology. 3. Wives—Conduct of life.
I. Title.

HQ734.S3783 2004
306.81—dc21
                                                                    2003049940
ISBN-10: 0-06-052062-0 (pbk.)
ISBN-13: 978-0-06-052062-5 (pbk.)

    14   NMSG/RRD   30   29   28   27   26   25   24   23   22   21

For family and friends who have stood by me—
in humble gratitude.

ACKNOWLEDGMENTS

Without the sensitive, honest, open, generous, and profound contributions of my audience—this book wouldn't have been possible. Thank you all for helping me help others.

Contents

AUTHOR'S NOTE

While the ideas, suggestions, and techniques offered in this book are going to improve your relationship with your husband (or yours with your wife if you get her to read this book), and your attitude about yourself, your marriage, and your life, it is important to qualify this enthusiastically optimistic perspective with a serious concern. As I wrote in my first book, *Ten Stupid Things Women Do to Mess Up Their Lives,* and reiterated in a later book, *Ten Stupid Things Couples Do to Mess Up Their Relationships,* the 3 A's: Addictions, Abuse, and Affairs, are behaviors, in my opinion, that break the covenant and justify the self-preserving decision to end the relationship. Where the behavior of one or both of the spouses is blatantly destructive, dangerous, or evil, this book does not apply.

The Proper Care and Feeding of Husbands has salvaged and revitalized innumerable strained, stagnant, boring, disappointing, annoying, frustrating, and even seemingly dead marriages, as the real-life examples happily demonstrate. I have had women calling almost daily, bitterly criticizing their men, reporting of months of seemingly useless marital therapy (aka "gripe hours"), and at their wits' end about what to do with their marriages. After I ask (well, really nag) them to try just *one* of the hints found in this book, such as finding one or two things to compliment their husbands about (no matter how small) each day for five days, they call me back amazed at the positive results in their feelings about their men, their husbands' demeanor, and the atmosphere in the home. They see progress! They feel powerful! They are happier! Their marriages are experienced as more of a blessing.

My deepest hope is that this book will bring that blessing to your home.

P.S. Reading this book may be of benefit to your health! According to biologists at the University of Pennsylvania, ". . . male perspiration had a surprisingly beneficial effect on women's moods. It helps reduce stress, induces relaxation, and even affects the menstrual cycle." (The *Orange County Register,* March 15, 2003.)

—Dr. Laura C. Schlessinger, 2003

INTRODUCTION

"As a man, I can tell you our needs are simple. We want to be fed, we want our kids mothered, and we want lovin'."
VINCE

"Men are only interested in two things: If I'm not horny, make me a sandwich."
JOHN

"I am a thirty-seven-year-old man who has seen quite a bit in life, and I can offer this to your search for how to treat a man. We are men, not dumb-dumbs, psychics, or one bit unromantic. We need only clear communication, appreciation, honest love, and respect. This will be repaid by laying the moon and stars at your feet for your pleasure. There is no need to 'work' a man to get what you want. We live to take care of a wife, family, and home. Just remember that we are men, and know that our needs are simple but not to be ignored. A good man is hard to find, not to keep."
DAN

"A good man is hard to find, not to keep." That sentence should really make you stop and think. As a radio talk-show host/psychotherapist, I've got to tell you how remarkably true and sad it is that so many women struggle to hold on to some jerk, keep giving an abusive or philandering man yet another chance, have unprotected sex with some guy while barely knowing his last name, agree to shack up and risk making babies with some opportunist or loser, all in a pathetic version of a pursuit for love, *but* will resent the hell out of treating a decent, hardworking, caring husband with the thoughtfulness, attention, respect, and affection he needs to be content. It boggles my mind.

What further puts me in boggle overdrive is how seemingly oblivious and insensitive many women are to how destructive they are being to their men and consequently to their marriages. Women will call me asking me if it's alright to go off on extended vacations "without *him*" when they want some freedom or R&R, or if it's okay to cut him off from sex because they're annoyed about something or just too tired from their busy day, or if they really have to make him a dinner when he gets home from work because it's just too tedious to plan meals, or if it's okay to keep stuff from him (like family or financial issues) because his input is unnecessary, or if they're really obligated to spend time with his family (in-laws or stepkids), or if they really have to show interest in his hobbies when they're bored silly by them, or—well, you get the idea.

Let me relate the specific call that prompted me to write this book. Annette is thirty-five, her husband is thirty-nine, and they have a one-year-old son. She is a stay-at-home mom who just doesn't enjoy cooking and doesn't feel it's useful to spend a lot of time doing it. She called wondering if that was detrimental or not to her child. Right away I was alerted to her lack of concern about the needs or desires of her husband—you know, the guy who slays dragons for her and their child every day. In order to really get a feel for this caller, you'll have to imagine the completely hostile and disdainful manner in which she spoke.

DR. LAURA: What do you do for food?

ANNETTE: We eat peanut-butter-and-jelly sandwiches.

DR. LAURA: That's not healthy three times a day.

ANNETTE: No, he's [the child] not eating it three times a day.

DR. LAURA: What do you eat for dinner?

ANNETTE: Well, he's still breast-feeding at one year old.

DR. LAURA: What do the adults in your house eat for dinner?

ANNETTE: My husband might eat beef enchiladas from the freezer, and I might eat cereal or cottage cheese. My husband doesn't much like what I cook.

DR. LAURA: That's not really a balanced, healthy diet. Are you intentionally making awful things that he won't eat or is he some kind of ogre?

ANNETTE: (Sarcastically) No, I'm just not a good cook. [What you can't read is her disdainful, hostile tone.]

DR. LAURA: Okay, Annette, being a better cook is easy to come by. All you do is take a class or get a book of recipes. I wonder if you're intentionally undermining his enjoyment of a home-cooked meal so that you simply don't have to do it. Let me tell you what is detrimental to your child. Dinnertime turns out to be one of the most important functions of a family in terms of a child bonding with parents, their ability to communicate and feel close to their parents—all of which supports their self-esteem. The dinner table is a most important aspect of that bonding. That is the routine time when the family sits down, says their prayers, and spends that pleasant time enjoying their meal together and talking. So, if that means you have to do what you don't like, so be it. Or did you plan to teach your son that when he doesn't enjoy something, he doesn't have to do it at all, or he doesn't have to do it right? In which case you are going to have a child growing up to be a monster.

There are a lot of things we all don't enjoy doing, but they are part of the rigor of life and they are a part of our obligations in our various roles. To be people of integrity, we have to follow through whether or not we enjoy something. So, if you are at home, I think it is important for you to make the effort to prepare pleasant dinners because I think that's part of the joy and comfort for your family. Put in the effort. If your husband can eat frozen, prepackaged Mexican food, with all those spices, it means he has a pretty open-minded stomach—so you must be going far out of your way to mess with him. I don't understand that hostility, especially from a woman who has a one-year-old child. The ability for you to maintain a safe and nurturing home for that child largely depends on the quality and existence of your marriage. I'd expect you to make more of an effort.

Most of the women who complain that they are not getting what they want from their husbands should stop and look at how disrespectful and disdainful they are of them. They should also look at what they put their time and energy into at the expense of him and their marriage. It would be a stunner for them to realize that they try harder to impress strangers than they try to impress the person who is supposed to be the most important to them. As one listener, Gary, says:

"A husband is like a horse. At the end of the day he is usually rode hard and put away sweaty. Like in the movies, if his

master drives and beats him, he'll go just so far before bucking and rebelling.

If you love him, if you coax him, he'll drive himself till his heart explodes before he will let down his master. He'll give himself to death for the one he loves.

Which way should women handle a man?"

I have never gotten a complaint from a male listener in twenty-five years on the radio over my assertion that men are very simple creatures. They agree. I have explained time and again on my radio program that men are borne of women and spend the rest of their lives yearning for a woman's acceptance and approval. Unless you've got a man with a frank mental or personality disorder (the exception, not the rule), men admittedly are putty in the hands of a woman they love. Give him direct communication, respect, appreciation, food, and good lovin', and he'll do just about anything you wish—foolish or not.

With one particular caller, Sandy, I pushed this agenda through to a successful conclusion—but not without a lot of sweat on my part and resistance on Sandy's part.

SANDY: My husband and I have a horrible relationship.

DR. LAURA: And why is that, I wonder.

SANDY: He says I'm too headstrong . . . but I think we are both too headstrong for each other.

DR. LAURA: He says you are too headstrong. And what does that mean?

SANDY: He always tells me I like to take over situations— that I like to control situations and that I go around him when we should discuss these things together. I just go ahead and do it myself.

DR. LAURA: So, why do you do that?

SANDY: I don't know.

DR. LAURA: It is destroying your marriage. Why would you continue to do that?

SANDY: But it is stupid things like going to the store and buying something. Why should I consult him in things like that?

DR. LAURA: Well, it doesn't hurt to have a chat or invite him to come along.

SANDY: I just don't see it.

DR. LAURA: Do we have kids in the middle of this?

SANDY: Yeah, we have three kids.

DR. LAURA: That is why we have to make changes—so that the three kids have a peaceful home. And you can make the changes.

SANDY: We worked on it.

DR. LAURA: No. *We* didn't work on it. *You* didn't change.

SANDY: It is just hard.

DR. LAURA: So what, it's hard. This is about the lives of your three children. Don't tell me something is difficult to do when your three kids are depending on it. That should be incredible motivation for you to behave better in your marriage—to treat your husband better in your marriage.

SANDY: Right.

To help her make some changes, I asked her to make a short list, right then and there while we were on air, of three reasonable things her husband wished she would do differently. She fought this tooth and nail. First, she supposedly didn't know what he'd want, then she complained about him, then she got sarcastic about his needs, then she exaggerated what she'd have to do. Whew! It was tough to get through the resistance to admit that any of his desires or requests were reasonable, much less show any willingness to give him something he wanted.

I explained to her that personal change was difficult, bitching about somebody else was easy. I persisted with my question, offering her the opportunity to make things better for herself and her children. Finally, she relented—well, sort of—you can still read the "edginess."

DR. LAURA: What are three reasonable things you know would please him if you changed?

SANDY: If I took his opinion on things. If I listen to what he says and do it.

DR. LAURA: Okay. That seems fair for a marriage. What else?

SANDY: He would like to see me accept him for the way he is without asking for any more.

DR. LAURA: Generally, I think that means he wants to feel appreciated for what he is and does.

SANDY: Right.

DR. LAURA: And, when you are constantly trying to change him or demand more or different, he reads that as though you don't approve and appreciate what he is offering and who he is. Remember, this *is* the man *you* picked. Okay? So he needs more appreciation. And, what is number three?

SANDY: To just let things slide off my back sometimes. He always says I am too perfect.

DR. LAURA: Okay. Be easier going.

SANDY: Right.

DR. LAURA: Here's your assignment. Do this for a few days and call me back. Number one is *ask him for his opinion about something.* Number two is *show him some appreciation.* Number three is *if it really isn't important, let it pass because nobody likes to be jumped on all the time.* Read them back to me please.

SANDY: Ask him his opinion. Show him appreciation. If it isn't real important, let it pass.

She did call back in a few days and was rather surprised that with seemingly small efforts she had helped to improve her husband's mood and behavior and lighten up the atmosphere in the home, all leading to her own peace of mind.

But that is what I keep telling women. Men are simple straight lines. Generally, unlike women, men do not have mercurial moods (like PMS) or hypersensitivity to interpersonal slights (when was the last time you heard a man complain about his *father*-in-law?). Men usually mean exactly what they say and don't speak in the more indirect style more typical of women. Also, men will typically suffer in silence long, long before they will complain or screech out in pain (isolation and alcohol abuse is where it shows), while women are more likely to use whining and complaining as a form of communication and even entertainment with their girlfriends.

Men are simple. They know it. Women have to learn it if they expect to be truly happy with their man.

Kathryn, another of my listeners, confirms this:

> *"Men really are not as complicated as we think they should be. Men love to hear that their woman is happy and that they are the source of this happiness. Men deserve the same respect you would show a visitor in your home—even more. Men love to be complimented. They also like to be admired. I always thank my husband for working so hard for us, and I encourage the kids to do so, too. Men are grumpy when they are tired and/or hungry. Anything they say while they are in either one of these states is not to be taken seriously. Men don't like it when women talk about them behind their backs. Men are not your 'daddies,' they are your contemporaries and get stressed and scared about things just like you do. And if you were a real friend, you would help ease their burdens, not add to them. Men have dreams, too, and it doesn't matter if it's logical or not, don't walk all over them.*

This doesn't mean that we don't have problems—everyone does—but it's a lot easier to work them out with a man who knows you love and respect him."

I have been sadly amazed by the lack of understanding and appreciation so many women demonstrate for those basic facts. A recent caller to my radio program took the cake with her call. She is married for the second time and they both have children from prior marriages. She is working full-time and is involved in all sorts of activities. She called to complain about her "demanding" husband. It seems he was unhappy in his new marriage because his wife, my caller, was not spending time with him in or out of bed. She described an unbelievably hectic daily schedule, remarking that she just had too much on her plate to have time or energy or impulse to be intimate at all, much less physically intimate, with her new husband.

I immediately suggested that she take a cosmic spoon and dump stuff off her plate to make room for her new marriage, for her husband, for their relationship. She immediately came back with, "But shouldn't he just be understanding?" I almost flipped! He should be understanding about being ignored, about being at the bottom of her priority list? I responded, "Why should he agree to be a boarder in his own home, with no effort at all from you for a personal relationship? Why should he be sanguine about that? Why should he be sympathetic to your choice to exclude him from your life?"

Her answer, so telling, was, "Ohhh. I didn't see it that way at all."

I reiterated that she had to dump much of what was she was *voluntarily* allowing to hog up her plate and make room for him, or he was going to dump her off *his* plate, and that I wouldn't blame him much at all.

These calls are *not* aberrant. They reflect truly typical attitudes of a preponderance of women in today's America. Since

Gloria Steinem wrote that "women need men like fish need bicycles," more than a generation of women have foolishly bought that destructive nonsense and have denigrated men, marriage, familial obligation, and motherhood—all to their own detriment. Normal, healthy women yearn to be in love, married, and raising children with the man of their dreams. However, when their own mothers, much less society, tell them that they don't need men to be happy, or to raise children, and that their own children don't even need a mother raising them (day care will do), it's caused many women to lose the incentive and the ability to treat their personal lives with the love, dedication, sacrifice, compassion, and loyalty that will ultimately bring them happiness and a sense of purpose.

Sonya, a listener, echoes biblical scriptures with her note:

"And at the end of the day . . . roll over in bed, close your eyes, give him a big hug, and remember that without him, you are only a sorry excuse for a person, but as half of the team, you are invincible."

In Genesis God said, "It is not good that man be alone; I will make him a helper corresponding to him. . . . Therefore a man shall leave his father and his mother and cling to his wife and they shall become one flesh."

Contrary to what a good forty years of feminist propaganda has claimed, it is not oppression, subjugation, or abdication of any feminine quality-of-life potential to marry a man, be proud of your bonding, rejoice in your gifts and sacrifices for your marriage and family, and derive pleasure and sustenance from your role as a wife and mother.

Your attitude makes all the difference in the quality of your life. And your understanding of men and what they dearly need will make all the difference in the quality of your marriage.

Kathy wrote:

"I told my husband about the book you are working on and asked him what he thought men want. He said, 'That's simple. Lots of sex and no nagging. What's so hard about that?'"

It's not quite that simple, but Kathy's husband's tongue-in-cheek answer speaks to the truth that women have all the power in the world to determine the behavior of their men. This power is released when women practice the *Proper Care and Feeding of Husbands.*

The Proper Care

and Feeding of Husbands

Chapter 1

THE *IM*PROPER CARE AND FEEDING OF HUSBANDS

"I laughed when I heard the title of your new book. I thought, 'It won't happen. What woman would buy it? Who cares about us men?' There are a few things that men want so bad they would do anything for it. I think a good number of men want respect more than love. They like to feel they have some power. I nearly cry when you tell a woman caller to respect her husband. There is so much selfishness in the world—in marriages. Prosperity has allowed women to be so independent, and thus so selfish. I always feel as though I come last—my feelings come last, my needs come last."

EDGAR

There isn't a day that goes by when I don't ask at least one woman caller on my radio program if she expects to stay married considering her hostile, dismissive, or undermining attitude and actions toward her husband. What is amazing is how surprised they all seem to imagine that their husbands might have a limit to how much they'll take before they tune out or turn away. What is even more amazing is that this *in*sensitivity to their husbands' needs and feelings goes hand in hand with a

*hyper*sensitivity about any action or reaction from the men—
reactions that are usually more than reasonable.

Here's just one example of such a caller from my radio program the day before I began writing this chapter. This
"Christian" woman has been married one year to a "Jewish"
man, and they have a four-month-old son. Before they married she promised to raise their children Jewish, even though,
obviously, neither one was truly invested in and committed to
their religion (because, if they were, they would have married
someone with whom they could share their faith). Now that it
is Christmastime, she put up a tree and is already revving up
for Easter egg hunts. "I don't want my children to miss out on
all the wonderful holiday experiences I had as a child," she says
to me by way of rationalizing her broken promise.

What was her question for me even after I reminded her of
her promise and vows? Of course it was, "How can I get him
to stop walking around angry and pouting?" That she
betrayed her vow was easily dismissed, I think, by the double
standard most women have about what they do and what their
men do. If women change their minds, men must take it.
When men change their minds, they're brutes.

One male listener wrote to me of his frustration with this
double standard. He lamented that women need to understand
how frustrating it is dealing with a double standard that only
takes into account the woman's immediate needs or desires. It
was his perception that everything the woman feels or needs is
legitimate and very important, while anything related to the
man is unimportant and selfish.

I think, as generalizations go, he has a good point. Try visit-
ing various female-oriented Internet chat rooms, and you'll
find cheering sections rallying behind women who trash their
men, determined to leave them for trivial reasons ("He's not
talkative enough," "I just don't feel complete," "I'm bored," or
"He doesn't want me talking to my mother every day").

And while we're talking about double standards, let's not forget what happens in the bedroom. Women expect their men to "understand" when they're not interested in sex, but when the men don't or can't perform—watch out!

What causes this double-standard mentality? In one big, hyphenated word: self-centeredness. And what is the source of this self-centeredness? I believe it's a result of the women's movement, with its condemnation of just about everything male as evil, stupid, and oppressive, and the denigration of female and male roles in families, as well as the loss of family functioning as a result of divorce, day care, dual careers, and the glorification of shacking up and unwed motherhood by choice. These are the core destructive influences that result in women not appreciating that they are perfected, as are men, when they are bonded in wedlock and have obligations to family.

The result is women get married thinking largely about what their marriage and their man can do for them, and not what they can do for their men. And when there is so little emphasis on the giving, the nitpicking and pettiness chews up and spits out what could have been a good marriage.

Cindy's e-mail addresses the issue of "giving" and "doing":

"I have been married for ten years and I had a huge problem with Caring and Feeding *my husband. I did not know the time my mother put into caring and feeding my dad until I was having difficulty in my marriage. It was then she helped me understand a wife's role. My generation (I'm in my 30s) was raised in a very 'me' culture: If we're not happy, then no one will be. Luckily, my mom and dad taught me that in order to be happy and fulfilled, you must help, love, and care . . . for others! Even with a great home life as a child, I didn't know that was so true in a marriage. I just thought you either have a great marriage or you don't—that somehow marriage existed outside your efforts.*

That was just one of my misassumptions. Another was that he should be as knowledgeable about things as my dad, with whom I constantly compared him. I constantly nagged instead of encouraged. Then my dad gave me advice on how the male ego worked. I followed his direction, being encouraging and essentially being his cheerleader. Things changed dramatically.

My mother's advice, after my many mess-ups, was to love him. Now, that sounds pretty basic, but I now truly understand what the word 'love' means. It's a profoundly tender, passionate affection for someone; an affectionate concern for their well-being. God's greatest gift, after life itself, is love. God created him for you. Love your husband with all your heart and treat him like the gift from God that he is."

The notion of love as a gift, as a verb, as an attitude, as a commitment, is a revelation to some. Unfortunately, love is usually looked at as a feeling that comes over you and makes you happy; and of course, *if* you're happy, *then* you behave nicely. Somehow, the notion is out there that you're entitled to behave badly if you don't feel that lovin' feeling. More than that, if you don't feel that lovin' feeling, you're entitled to get it somehow, somewhere, with someone else who's available. This sense of entitlement comes from a culture that has elevated feelings over obligation, responsibility, and commitment.

"I have a right to be happy, don't I?" is not an infrequent comment from callers frustrated that their marriages haven't put them in a perpetual Valium-drip state. And this focus on happiness helps them to rationalize their virtual abandonment of marriage and family, and their replacing it with hobbies, drugs and alcohol, work, affairs, whining in therapy or with friends or family, or hostility directed at those who love them.

This is not a minor issue. When marriages are distressed, the children are hurt and limited in their ability and hope to achieve happiness. This is the point I bring to the attention of many women callers who, with unrealistic demands and outrageously negative behaviors, determine that the solution to the problems in their home is divorce. There are two issues that I force them to look at. The first is that children of divorce will suffer both in the present and in the future. The second is that they are wrong if they think a new pair of pants will change their lives—because the same skirt will be in the room!

I challenge them to do what they complain their spouses won't or can't do: change! I explain that men are indeed simple creatures, and if you change certain aspects of your interaction, like magic you will see changes in them, too. I remind them that their current feelings do not need to change before they can change their behavior. I ask them to behave "as if" things were lovely in their relationship: a call of affection during the day, a kiss at the door, a nice outfit when at home, a request for his opinion about something to do with the family, a comment of appreciation for something well done, a hug, a good meal, a back rub, some alone time after work before dealing with plumbing or financial problems, and a cuddle at bedtime . . . which might get even more interesting.

Invariably, the women protest. Why should they have to be nice when things aren't exactly the way they want them? Clifford, a listener, e-mailed about this attitude:

> "What ever happened to sweetness? If you act like a Bi*ch, you will be treated like a Bi*ch. I asked my wife once if she wanted something, as she was being unusually nice. She angrily said to me 'I would never be nice to anyone to get them to do something for me. That is sucking up!'
>
> So, what is the alternative? Treat them like Sh*t? A man takes care of his woman and a woman should take care of her man! What a concept!"

What surprised me when I went to my Web site (www. drlaura.com), where I'd asked listeners to send me contributions for this book, was the avalanche of expressed pain from husbands—not so much anger, but pain. It may be a surprise for many women to imagine that their husbands are in pain because of their behavior toward them. In all fairness, men do tend to be more stoic than women; they try to be strong and carry on no matter what. I do not fault that at all. That is a description of masculinity, one that has been under attack from a feminized culture that denies the importance of such inner strength and fortitude. Without those and other masculine characteristics, much of Western civilization would not have evolved. Think about the self-control and self-denial necessary in exploration or combat or survival under ferocious conditions. I do believe that it's to the betterment of men and society that women temper and civilize these masculine characteristics; however, to deny the reality and value of masculine traits altogether is cruel toward boys and men, not to mention foolish, as it undermines the home and country.

That men do not emote pain, hurt, and despair like women do seems to mean to some women that men are not feeling anything. The truth is men suck it up and just try to get along in life in general and with us in particular. Women should not measure or interpret a man's heart, soul, intent, or feelings based upon their own reactions. Women cry and talk; men don't ruminate on feelings, they try to do something about the situation. I guess that makes men lousy "girlfriends," but very helpful "partners" if women would respect their uniqueness.

Ray, a listener, signed himself "Frustrated and depressed husband":

> *"I hear many of the calls from women who sound so much like my wife. Their disdain for their obligations to their husbands is far too familiar. It is agonizing to listen and to know that I live with the indifference of a woman just like those callers.*
>
> *I can't describe the frustration, depression, and finally, the*

utter despair that is the result of twenty-four years of neglect. I can't do justice to the efforts that I have made to salvage a relationship that should be the cornerstone of our family, but is instead a millstone around my neck. I can't explain to you the progression from loving and nurturing husband, through concerned and understanding spouse, to frustrated and repressed male, and angry, depressed curmudgeon, all the way to desperate wretch.

Just know that you must write this book. If you can save just one family, you must write this book."

Ray was not alone in his lamentation. Too many men are living in this pain, having given up any hope of happiness after making every attempt to give their wives what they say they want so that they will treat their husbands nice.

What do women want?

Jill, a listener, sent me this Internet "joke" about "The Perfect Husband":

"A new Perfect Husband Shopping Center opened where a woman could go to choose from among many men to find the perfect husband. It was laid out on five floors, with the men increasing in positive attributes as you ascended the floors. The only rule was that once you open the door to any floor, you must choose a man from that floor, and if you go up a floor, you can't go back down except to leave the store. So, a couple of girlfriends go to the store to find a man to marry.

The first-floor sign reads: 'These men have high-paying jobs and love kids.' The women read the sign and say, 'Well, that's wonderful . . . but,' and wonder what's on the next floor.

The second-floor sign reads: 'These men have high-paying jobs, love kids, and are extremely good looking.' 'Hmmm,' say the girls. 'Wonder what's further up?'

The third-floor sign reads: 'These men have high-paying

jobs, love kids, are extremely good looking, and will help with the housework.' 'Wow!' say the women. 'Very tempting . . . but there's more further up!'

The fourth-floor sign reads: 'These men have high-paying jobs, love kids, are extremely good looking, will help with the housework, and are great in bed.' 'Oh, mercy me. But just think! What must be awaiting us further up?!' say the women.

So, up to the fifth floor they go.

The fifth-floor sign reads: 'This floor is just to prove that women are impossible to please.'"

Oops.

Here's an example of "I love you . . . now change into my perfect husband":

DR. LAURA: Nikki, welcome to the program.

NIKKI: I would like to know when it is appropriate for me to butt into my fiancé's life and when it isn't.

DR. LAURA: Why is it you think you have to butt into his life in many different arenas? You don't like him as he is?

NIKKI: I love him as a person, but there are certain things, like manners, he wasn't brought up with. His parents were hippies and let him do whatever he wanted. When I met him and we were walking across the street and I had high heels on and it was in the middle of winter, he didn't try to help me across the street.

DR. LAURA: In the dead of winter why were you walking around in high heels in the first place if you couldn't walk normally in them?

NIKKI: We were out to a fancy dinner.

DR. LAURA: People can wear sensible shoes no matter where they go. Okay, so you wore silly shoes and he didn't throw you over his shoulder.

NIKKI: What about such things as manners? When he

comes over to my parents' house and he puts his face about an inch from the food and says, 'Wow, this smells really great!'?

DR. LAURA: I think that is very complimentary.

NIKKI: Even if his face was right above the food?

DR. LAURA: Well, how else would he smell it?

NIKKI: I don't know. . . . Okay.

DR. LAURA: Nikki, if you are ashamed of him, get rid of him. If you are ashamed of him, leave him alone.

NIKKI: I'm not ashamed of him. Nobody is perfect. I am totally in love with him. What about him working out and eating better?

DR. LAURA: Nikki, get a different man. Stop beating this one to death. I am really sad that you pick a guy, say you are totally in love with him, but keep pointing out how he is totally unsatisfactory to you. That is insulting. That is not love. If you want an exercise maniac who reads Ms. Manners, get one of those. It is offensive and demoralizing to men when we women types grab on to them and then want to remold them in our image of the perfect man or perfect husband.

NIKKI: That is true.

DR. LAURA: It doesn't make them feel better about themselves.

NIKKI: Yeah, he does feel horrible about himself when I do that.

DR. LAURA: How cruel are you being? How nuts is he to keep taking it?

NIKKI: True. He doesn't have much self-esteem, so he just kind of takes it.

DR. LAURA: There must be a reason you want this kind of situation with a man. I don't know, maybe it gives you a sense of superiority.

NIKKI: I'm sure that's part of the problem.

Ouch. That problem is a frequent one, especially with women overmarinated in the most negative beliefs of the women's movement—that is, that society and men will oppress; they are the enemy; do not submit; terminate or dominate. And men are easily dominated with negativity from their woman. As I pointed out earlier, since men are simple creatures who come from a woman, are nurtured and brought up by a woman, and yearn for the continued love, admiration, and approval from a woman, it makes them vulnerable to their woman's moods, desires, tantrums, criticisms, disappointments, dissatisfactions, angers, and rejections.

Women need to better appreciate the magnitude of their power and influence over men, and not misuse or abuse it. Ladies, it won't make you happier.

One of the most typical ways that a wife misuses power over her husband is by her angry disappointment. Michelle, a listener, expressed this so well:

> *"My husband and I have been married for ten years. When we first married I started to watch soap operas. I expected my husband to treat me like the lovers of the soap opera stars were treated—without the cheating, of course. I blamed my husband for my unhappiness. If I was unhappy, I expected him to drop everything to make me happy. If he took me to dinner, I would feel neglected because he did not buy me flowers. My friends would readily agree with me that I was neglected and should not have to pick up his dirty socks off the floor. I was miserable and so was he.*
>
> *I went to a religious women's retreat where we were required to go to a marriage class. God showed me how selfish I was. I learned that my happiness was dependent upon me and not my husband. I learned that my friends should not be a sounding board for my frustrations with my marriage. They always encouraged me to be against my husband.*

I have found that most of my griefs are selfish and unwarranted. The ones that are not selfish I tell my husband about lovingly, and I don't nag. I am patient and he does fix it."

I agree that many women get tripped up when they try to measure their husbands' love by what the media or their friends tell them it should look like instead of by the husbands' own unique actions. One listener wrote that she had gotten all revved up for something incredible to happen for her on Valentine's Day. After hearing romantic, over-the-top stories from her friends about what their husbands had done, she expected her husband to sum up his feelings for her in similar grand fashion on this one day. And for five consecutive Valentine's Days, she was ferociously let down and disappointed. Not surprisingly, it showed in her behavior toward him in the subsequent weeks—without him knowing why.

Finally she expressed her annoyance. He devastated her by saying, "I show you I love you three hundred and sixty-five days a year, but if this one day isn't perfect, then none of that counts?" She felt like a complete jerk because she knew he was right. She remembered all the times he'd surprised her with flowers "just because," or took her on a surprise overnight trip, or spontaneously grabbed her in the kitchen and told her all the reasons he loved her.

She realized her husband loved her genuinely and that trying to force him to express it in a way that was more synthetic, while simultaneously discounting all he had done to show his love, was selfish and cruel. She wrote:

"I think if women would stop and pay attention, they would see that their husbands may not have stopped courting them but are actually doing it in a different way. It could be by getting up first when the baby cries, or doing the dishes so she can rest, or making a special dinner. Without acknowledging the more

*subtle ways our husbands show us they love us, we rob ourselves
and them of that connection. When their efforts are ignored long
enough, isn't it inevitable that they'll eventually stop?"*

I remember one fax to my radio program from a woman
whose husband had died. She commented that she saw a lot of
her friends complaining and whining about stupid stuff in
their marriages. She reflected on how these women didn't
realize how lucky they were to have those little problems in
their lives and that they should be happy to have someone to
care for and worry over. In short, they lacked gratitude for
what they had.

Kaye, a listener, sent me this e-mail to express her awaken-
ing to the notion of gratitude:

*"I must say that an important turning point for me came when
I was listening to you on the radio, Dr. Laura. You were listening to some woman grouse about picky little things, and you
asked her, 'Does your husband provide well for your family?
Are your kids all healthy? Do you get to stay at home with
them?' And so forth. She answered yes to all those questions.
Then you said, 'So stop whining! You have forgotten to be
grateful.'*

*It was as though God took me by the shoulders and said,
'Hello! This is you, idiot!' Right at that moment, in the car, I
began to thank God for my husband and for every excellent
quality he has. Since then, I have made a conscious effort to do
the following things:*

- *Thank God daily for such a terrific guy, mentioning specific
  qualities for which I'm grateful.*

- *Look for daily ways to be a blessing to my husband (trying to
  understand what pleases him, anticipating his needs, etc.).*

- *Chart my menstrual cycle and remind myself on the PMS days that what I'm feeling isn't true and to keep my mouth shut and let it pass.*

- *Avoid books, magazines, and TV shows that describe what marriage, family, and husbands ought to be like, and make a conscious effort to be grateful for things as they are instead of trying to change the people around me.*

- *Take responsibility for my own emotional well-being: Stay rested, don't overcommit and then complain, stay in touch with friends with a positive influence.*

- *Stay focused on making a home for my family and remember that this is my highest calling and responsibility, and that it has eternal value. The more I do this, the happier and more content I am."*

It is exciting to receive such letters, showing how a change in attitude, and a commitment to quality actions, can bring such deep, profound joy.

I spend hours of my radio program trying to help folks get past the frighteningly pervasive diabolical message that married women at home with the children somehow aren't total women, maximizing their potential, and that men are idiotic, self-centered sex fiends, incapable of contributing anything of value to women or children.

Chapter 2

THE WHITE RABBIT SYNDROME

"And at the end of each day . . . relax. Let it all go; tomorrow will be there whether you worry or not—so let it go. Kiss each other, even if the kids can see. They need it, too."

SUZANNE

"I'm late, I'm late, for a very important date. No time . . ." was the retort of the White Rabbit when Alice was trying to ask him for help in Lewis Carroll's *Alice in Wonderland*. Sadly, this is the same retort many wives give their husbands, who are eager to make an intimate connection. Astonishing.

One of my listeners, Marie, wrote a letter to me detailing her slip down that rabbit hole:

"The best pointer I could give to wives about the care and feeding of a husband is to always make time for him. I know wives and moms get so, so, so, so busy. I do not know how I kept up with the soccer games, baseball practices, Scouts, and piano lessons—not to mention dinner, laundry, and an occasional trip to the grocery store or vet. I don't know how I did it."

She then told the story of one particular day, a day like all other days in that it was filled with errands and activities. But this day was different. This day was her husband's birthday. And she had completely forgotten. No cake. No gift. No card. No acknowledgment at all. She only realized that it was his birthday when his mother stopped over, as she did every year on her son's birthday, to drop off this year's plaid shirt, and innocently asked if she was too late for the cake.

Even her children were mad at her. What did her husband do? *He* comforted *her* when she started crying in embarrassment and frustration!

"This is a man who works seven A.M. to seven P.M. five days a week and seven A.M. to twelve P.M. on Saturday so that I can be home with the kids. He certainly deserved better."

That night, her mother-in-law, who rarely "got involved," told her that she had better take care of the person she had decided to spend the rest of her life with, or when the children were grown up and out of the house, she would be alone.

"Of course, she was right. I got so wrapped up in the daily stuff to do that I was not taking care of the great guy who was taking care of me. I started making a point of putting him higher on my list of priorities, and suddenly I was feeling like a wife again and not a frazzled mom.

I started the very next day with a little love letter in his lunch box. I got a phone call in the middle of the day when he read it. We started exchanging smiles over the dinner table while the kids went on about their day, and it was so nice to get to know this really great guy I had picked.

All marriages have ups and downs, but if you stay focused on why you got married in the first place, you can't lose."

If the only conclusion drawn from this episode is that the wife now has more to take care of or fret about, larger points have been missed. For example, the outcome for Marie was more pleasure and more peace. Having that loving, attentive, playful connection with her husband *reduced* stress by adding a dimension of shared joy. This is a point too many women miss when they complain about being drained by their husbands' needs, or when they resent their husbands' needs, or when they perceive themselves as being victimized by their lives.

Which brings me to my next point, which is that lives are constructed of choices. Unless lightning has struck your house (obviously out of your control), your life is constructed out of the building blocks of your choices, good ones as well as bad. The bad choices (self-centered, shortsighted, immature, or just plain stupid) can have unpleasant consequences to marriages.

There are only so many hours in a day and only so many things any of us can do and still do well. Prioritizing is a must. Without it—that is, without formally or informally listing in order of importance what is necessary and what is negotiable—the important things tend to slip down on the list. Prioritizing is a moment-to-moment necessity, not just an issue of long-term planning.

Luke, a listener, wrote to me of a call he heard on my program that changed his immediate behavior. The caller had asked what she could do about her husband, who felt that he wasn't the number one priority in her life. I quickly told her that she needed to make him the number one priority or, in essence, her marital vows were hollow. Of course, she resisted, complaining about already having too many demands on her and this just made her life tougher. I commented on how self-centered a perspective that was and challenged her to imagine being on the receiving end of her behavior.

After hearing this, Luke wrote:

"I was thinking about how crazy it is to marry and then not enjoy it with your spouse. My wife and I have been married for just under a year, and I really enjoy marriage.

Then I began to reflect on what my weekend held, and you guessed it: I was about to neglect our 'Friday Date Night' in the name of studying for my college finals and my lesson preparation for my high-school teaching job. Well, my wife was still at work when I got home, so I got out the books and tried to get as much done as possible. When she walked in the door, I hugged her and told her to get ready because we were going out on the town that night."

Luke admitted that he had been letting her slip on his priority list—and that it hadn't even taken a year for him to become a meathead. He had justified this priority shuffling with the thought that he would put his wife at number one when he had more time. He ended his letter by thanking me for the lesson learned that no one is immune to occasional shortsightedness and faulty logic.

It is important to look again at what that logic was: that he would put her at #1 when he had more time. What does that mean? That means that she was never to be #1 unless there was nothing else on the list. When was that going to happen?

Julie, a listener, related the truth about what "doing for" a husband actually does for the wife:

"Even if I am having a long day, too, I can pick up deli sandwiches, a container of soup, and some parsley. Planning my evening surprise for my husband, strangely, takes away my stresses at work as well, because I am thinking about someone else.

At home, I cut the sandwiches into triangles, stick fancy toothpicks through them, pour soup into bowls and add some garnish, set the table, and then greet him at the door with a big kiss and hug.

How much time did this take? Five extra minutes. How much did we both receive? I had the opportunity to say in a small way, 'We are a team and I support you,' and he felt good that I had taken the extra time to make a simple thing beautiful just for him."

How beautiful is that? She didn't even have to wait to get goodies of gratitude back from him in order to feel good; she felt good simply from the giving. That put feeling good in her control. Get it?

Unfortunately, too many women fail to see their marriages as a source of satisfaction and accomplishment in the way they've been led to believe their careers will be. One caller, Suzanne, forty-three years old and married for more than twenty years, actually demonstrated hostility toward her husband's desire to spend time with her.

SUZANNE: Hi, Dr. Laura. I am a real estate agent, which is an all-or-none profession. I have been in it for about five years. I have just started to build up my career, and this past weekend, my husband gave me the ultimatum of either quitting my job or he wants a divorce.

DR. LAURA: Why?

SUZANNE: (laughing) Because he feels neglected on weekends and evenings.

DR. LAURA: What if he was neglecting you on nights and weekends? Wouldn't you be in some women's group bitching about it? Every time I see a movie with a group of women, they're complaining bitterly about how their men are all focused on their work or something else and aren't paying attention to them. So when we do it to them, it is called . . . what?

SUZANNE: Well, I feel like I earned where I am right now.

DR. LAURA: He feels like he earned the respect of a married person.

SUZANNE: I followed him overseas for five years.

DR. LAURA: This is an ugly payback for something you probably agreed to do. I can't imagine being married to someone I wouldn't see on the evenings or weekends. Suzanne, you are probably going to be divorced. The message you are giving him is that being a real-estate agent means more to you than being married to him. He has warned you. I think you are a foolish woman. With the expertise, knowledge, and talent you have, there are challenging things you could do during the week, and keep evenings and weekends for family time. If family means nothing to you, you will lose it. Your man, in my opinion, is not making any unreasonable demands. And after all these years, and all your nonsense, he still loves you and wants to be your man. At your age of forty-three, see how many other guys are going to say that to you, sweetheart.

I can't understand why a wife would see her husband wanting to spend time with her as a bad thing. They have been married twenty-something years and he still wants to be with her? That's a huge compliment!

This is not about controlling her. This is about wanting to have a life with her. How sad that she might not see that in time.

This mentality is the ugly part of the feminist movement, which supports personal success, acquisition, accomplishment, power, and the feminist political agenda over love, marriage, and family. When Karen Hughes, a counselor to President Bush, decided to resign to move back to Texas and spend more time with her family, many feminist spokes-types accused her of selling out women. Hmmm . . . what ever happened to "choice"?

Ms. Hughes and millions of other women have made the choice to give up their all-consuming careers. Why? Largely because the feminist battle cry of "having it all" resulted in lots of stress over a myriad of competing demands for time, guilt for the virtual neglect of children, and longing for more home-and-hearth time. In fact, there is even a new syndrome ascribed to working mothers called "Hurried Woman Syndrome," a term coined by some in the medical community who listened to women's complaints about their busy lifestyles.

This syndrome has been defined by the symptoms of weight gain, low sex drive, moodiness, and fatigue—all due to the stress caused by trying to do too much, not being able to keep up with it, not feeling very accomplished at any of it, resenting anyone who has any expectations (like husband and children), and ending up feeling hostile and depressed.

Cheryl, a listener, sent me a news release about this and added her own thoughts:

> "In this world of 'do-it-all moms,' the ones who have babies, jobs, and every activity imaginable for their children, it is not surprising that the medical community has a newly diagnosed 'disease' for women. How does the medical community plan on 'curing' this new disease? Just a little something to think about."

So much of the mail I receive from young women tells me a terrible story about how they feel compelled to look at life in only one way, and that way leads them to minimize the value of family and marriage to their souls and psyches at the same time they maximize their drive for financial conquest, thanks to the messages of society, the choices of their friends, and even the pressures of their own families. They tell me how they are made to feel foolish, weak, and stupid for wanting to raise their own children (instead of using nannies and day care), or for working only part-time outside of the home, if at all (instead of having equal fiscal strength to their husbands)— even for yearning for marriage at all (instead of shacking up or having babies on their own).

These women tell me how their own mothers or mothers-in-law deride them for being "lazy" for being stay-at-home moms rather than having careers, and how their own girl-friends demean them for wanting to marry and take care of their man, and they talk of the loneliness they feel in their neighborhoods because so few of their compatriots share their family-directed values.

And so the women who choose to focus their lives on family are marginalized, while the women who choose to "have it all" end up with Hurried Woman Syndrome. Generally, the HWS women do not treat their children or husbands well at all. Why? Because when you're tired and stressed out by the requirements of a job you must fulfill (or risk being fired), you tend to make everyone else pay the price (even strangers in traffic) because you have nothing else to give.

I remember just such a woman from my private-practice days. She was married, with one young adolescent boy. She came to her counseling session in her lovely business suit and polished pumps, and with a well-worn attaché case. She paced angrily, furious that her husband had the temerity to ask for some time alone to talk with her when she came through the door after work.

"Doesn't he have any respect?" she fumed. "Doesn't he understand I'm tired from a tough day and I just don't need any more demands on me?"

I looked at her quietly for a moment, then barely whispered, "Yes to number one, no to number two." She stared at me for the longest time, then started up again with her complaints about his insensitivity and selfishness.

Again, I looked at her quietly for a moment, then barely whispered, "*His* insensitivity and selfishness?"

She sat down and started to cry.

Many married women with children are wearing themselves down to the point that ill health and ill temper are the result. The problem is not with the demands of their husbands and children; the problem is with their notion of a full life. "Having it all" begins to approximate a "jack of all trades and a master of none." It is also a self-perpetuating trap. If the work is demanding and draining, and your time is limited and your temper isn't, guilt usually drives one toward more activity for children to "make up" for the neglect and mistreatment. That translates into frenetic schedules of extracurricular activities, which end up overextending and stressing the children as well as the parents. Fast-food dinners on the fly start substituting for healthy, nutritious, joyous, intimate family dinners, resulting in isolation as family members all do "their own thing."

And since the husband is an adult, he's just left to his own devices or attacked as a nuisance for his reasonable expectations for a love life and home life.

I get too many calls from women complaining that their husbands' unreasonable, selfish, insensitive, and annoying demands on a "tired woman" amount to mental abuse! Oh, please!

Tina, forty-six, called with her husband, Jerry, fifty-six. Jerry began the discussion by outlining their debate about the number of times marital intimacy should occur in a marriage:

JERRY: I am saying that for a good, healthy relationship, there is nothing wrong with us making love at least three times a week. She thinks once or twice every two or three weeks is a healthy relationship. I said we

should call Dr. Laura because she knows what is
healthy and what isn't.

DR. LAURA: Thanks for the endorsement. Tina, you heard
what Jerry said. Is that a reasonable rendition of the
issue?

TINA: Yes, yes, that is pretty close.

DR. LAURA: Did you ever like to have sex more than you
do now?

TINA: Well, it isn't that I don't like it. When Jerry and I
were first married, it was a lot.

DR. LAURA: So, what, has it gotten boring?

TINA: Maybe a little boring. But, more important, I am
tired a lot.

DR. LAURA: Tina, that is not a fair excuse. It is your *obligation* to keep yourself healthy and fit so that you can be
involved with your husband. You can't do the "I am
tired" bit every day and have your husband just accept
that this important, intimate part of his life is simply
going to be controlled by your whim. It is your obligation not to be tired all the time. So take a nap, eat
more protein, take your vitamins. What kind of thing
is that to pull on him? What if he said, "I'm too tired
and I'm not going to work anymore"? You have obligations to each other, and one of them is not to be
constantly tired. That is not an acceptable excuse.
Now, if the lovemaking has gotten dull, what have you
done to spice it up?

TINA: (somewhat disdainfully) What have *I* done?

DR. LAURA: Yes, Tina, what have you done to spice it up?

TINA: Why do I have to do anything?

DR. LAURA: (shocked) Because you are one of the two
people having sex.

TINA: Well, sometimes I do the candles, but my complaint is that especially during the week, we both
have pretty high-pressured jobs.

DR. LAURA: Tina, your husband isn't complaining that his high-pressured job is leading him to neglect or reject you. Any woman who allows all her other choices of how she is spending her time to interfere with the love and intimacy with her husband is behaving like a fool. Your schedule is too intense for you and you should change it. Your commitments outside your marriage are too much for you. This is making you somewhat hostile and negative to the intimacy that is a great joy and a blessing in a relationship. Also, men need to feel the approval, acceptance, and attachment from their women that comes from sexual intimacy.

TINA: Okay.

DR. LAURA: So that *is* your obligation. It is not to spend yourself all at work.

TINA: (laughing) Yeah, I gave at the office. . . .

DR. LAURA: (laughing) You married him because you loved him and you wanted to make him happy.

TINA: Yes.

DR. LAURA: And I haven't heard too many women express being made unhappy by great orgasms with their husbands. Orgasms will put a smile on your face . . . and release a lot of tension.

There it is. If you decide that the most important thing about your life is your worker-ant role, you'll likely feel drained a lot of the time and resent the obligations you have to your husband and children—obligations that, ironically, will save you from that feeling of being drained in the first place. You are not loved, adored, and intimately needed at work. Check out all the competitive backbiting, layoffs, and computerization and mechanization substitutions for human beings going on in the workplace. Meanwhile, you are a goddess to your children and a queen to your husband. Let's see. Aside from the paycheck issue, which one is more nourishing and rewarding?

Now let me make something completely clear. I am not suggesting married women should not work. I am not suggesting that there is no valid form of personal expression of creativity and special gifts outside the home. Obviously, I have a radio and writing career. I just took up sailing. I love taking on challenges and doing service. But from day one, I have always made it clear to everyone, especially my husband and child, that if anything got in the way of family, it would get tempered or excised. It's one thing to have a tiring, stressful day—or even week. It's another thing to allow outside activities, no matter how seemingly important, to routinely get in the way of obligations to the roles created by holy vows, moral obligations, and love.

Caroline, a listener, learned this lesson and won the spiritual lottery:

> *"One day, after having a rough day at work, coming home to cook, clean, bathe kids, tend to my husband's needs, I told my husband I was too stressed out and he told me to quit my job. And he was serious. He didn't like to see me so stressed out trying to find someone to watch the kids, or just not having enough time to do the endless tasks a wife/mother needs to do.*
>
> *When I made the decision to quit my job, it was not only for the sake of my children, but also to support my husband, who works very hard. I now cook almost every meal during the week as opposed to putting something in the microwave or going to a fast-food joint. I used to ask my husband, 'How did I used to do it? Working full time, going to kids' sporting events, church events, personal life, etcetera,' and he replied, 'You didn't.' "*

The usual way the liberally biased media handles the issue of overextended women is to further condemn men for not picking up the slack at home—for letting their wives take on most of the burden of cleaning, cooking, and raising the children. First of all, it just isn't true—men do and always have helped out. Yes, I know the very phrase "helped out" makes a lot of feminists furious, but that's because they don't see men and women as having different temperaments, needs, attitudes, physiology, or psychology; they see a unisex world. And yet that world exists only in their naive imaginations. In the real world of humans, women have a unique urge toward bonding and nesting and nurturing. Men have a unique urge toward protecting, providing, and conquering. That doesn't mean men can't nurture children or that women can't climb mountains, but it does mean that beneath individual variations in constitution and temperament, women and men are different. Compatibility and harmony are best served when that difference is respected and, yes, even enjoyed, instead of denied or degraded.

Many talented, exceptional women have found that when their feet are firmly planted on family, their creativity has a comfortable place from which to soar. The day before I wrote this page, I received a novel and a letter from a newly published mystery author, Kathleen Antrim. Here is part of the letter she included with her novel, *Capital Offense*:

> "I feel I have just graduated from the Dr. Laura School of Life. My husband and I decided that when we had children, I would stay at home with them. So when we had our first child, I quit my career in sales and marketing. I'm a staunch believer that you can put your children and family first and still follow your personal dreams! I'm living proof."

Now, a word of caution. A wife's feet can be *too* firmly entrenched in only *one* part of family. Lynda, a listener, admits to this problem:

"The most important thing I have learned about the care and feeding of husbands, after three failures, is that God knew what He was talking about when He said 'forsaking all others' in Genesis. We women forget that, especially when the children come along. I was oblivious to the need to do this when I was married to the father of my children for seventeen years. We seldom went anywhere 'alone' together, and I totally ignored his needs. I always felt my children and their needs came first. I could never put him first."

Literally hundreds of men have written to me about their pain with being marginalized after the children were born. Once their wives became mothers, they had no time to be wives. The men would even compliment their wives on being great mothers, but expressed considerable pain over not being shown love, affection, or sexual interest. The typical reply from a wife challenged with this was "I only have time to take care of one person, and our child is that person. I'm just too tired for you."

This puts fathers in the ugly and uncomfortable position of feeling competitive with and resentful of their children, whom they love so much. They miss the affection, companionship, and lovemaking they used to share with their wives. They feel put aside and shut out and unimportant.

And then, of course, once this pattern is established, the wives call me complaining that their husbands aren't givin' and doin' what they want them to. No kidding.

Here's a call from one of those women, Lynn.

LYNN: I have a twenty-two-month-old daughter and I am her mother one hundred and ten percent. On Mother's Day, my husband didn't do anything for me—no card, nothing. So I'm still feeling pretty resentful.

DR. LAURA: What's he mad at?

LYNN: I don't know.

DR. LAURA: What would be your guess?

LYNN: Well, I asked him last night, and maybe he feels that he doesn't get enough attention, or that my focus is more on my daughter, but . . .

DR. LAURA: In other words, he's neglected by you, so he's not motivated to please you. Ma'am, it's a very simple matter. Some women tend to get very self-centered when they have babies. They begin to think that their babies are the center of the universe, and their husbands are just supposed to hang out like Uranus and keep revolving around you whether or not they're getting anything back. Doesn't work that way. People start getting rejected, they start feeling alienated. With men, that makes them unmotivated to be romantic back on your schedule.

LYNN: Well, it's hard to snuggle up to a man, though, who hasn't given you a Valentine's Day acknowledgment.

DR. LAURA: That is the consequence of ignoring your man.

LYNN: Okay.

DR. LAURA: Instead of getting on your high horse about not getting a crummy present, take this as a sign that you'd better start treating him like your man if you want him to treat you like his woman. Just because you gave birth doesn't entitle you to ignore your man. And you probably don't pay him ten percent of the attention you paid to him when you were dating.

LYNN: Probably not. So I have to be the one to break the cycle? Is that what you are saying?

DR. LAURA: You're the only one with the power to break the cycle.

She then worried aloud that if she broke the cycle by returning to being loving and attentive, he might not change his behavior toward her, and that would hurt her feelings. The truth is, men forgive just about anything when we women treat them well. They definitely do not hold on to grudges with the tenacity that most women do. Remember, men are simple creatures and very dependent upon their wives for acceptance, approval, and affection. When those 3 A's are restored, all is well in their world.

Connie, another listener, wrote to me, explaining that the "I'm too busy with the kids to love my man" excuse never entered her lexicon. She said that she had gotten the advice to always make her husband know he was the most important person in her life from a male friend who had divorced his "perfect wife" after twenty-five years of marriage. She related that he complained, "When I got home from work, they were all too busy to notice. . . ."

Ken, a listener, pointed out that many wives have a blind spot; that is, "once they become mothers, they fall into a rut and become their husband's second mother." This "second mother" mentality entails "looking like" and "sounding like" a mother on a tear! Ken went on:

> "They run around in 'mother attire' all the time rather than what they used to when they were out fishing for 'father,' and this continual visual turns most men off or pushes them else- where. . . . Not only do many wives look like mother most of the time, they move about the home constantly in mother mode: barking out orders, directing traffic, and beating the family drum. While this is all well and good, they forget to slip into wife mode, woman mode, lover mode, companion mode during private moments with their husbands."

Women have long complained that their men bring their work home both in their briefcases and in their heads. Likewise, then, a woman should also be alert not to always be obsessed with domestic and mundane issues when she reconnects with "her man" at the end of their mutually challenging and tiring day.

I often hear angry neofeminists whine that it is oppressive that society (read: men) expects women to flit around with the perfect body: no fat, no wrinkles, and no gray hair. Frankly, there are some superficial men for whom that is true, but the vast majority of men feel that attitude, demeanor, and behavior take a front seat to perfect skin. When a wife *behaves* sexily, handles herself *alluringly,* and by the way she *looks* at her husband, *touches* him, and *talks* to him conveys her interest, love, respect, and attraction, frankly, he'll go anywhere and do anything and slay all dragons for his family. On the other hand, if she's too busy whipping him into shape so that her world is ordered, and she forgets to be his companion, his lover, his woman, then he'll forget Valentine's Day, anniversaries, and birthdays. Not hard to understand, is it?

Evan, a listener, confirms this reality:

> *"[My wife] feels that if she doesn't remind me again and again, something won't get done. But the fact is, it makes me feel like her child and that Mommy needs to check up on me. It's degrading. I want to be admired. I want to be acknowledged for being the breadwinner and making sure that we are all well taken care of. My greatest pleasure is when I feel like her hero. Like her 'man.' Not her boy."*

As one caller once quipped on my radio program, "My mother always said, 'You had a husband before you had children—don't forget it!'"

It cannot be emphasized enough that sometimes the wife's field of interest becomes so overwhelmingly filled with obligations to her family that she loses sight of her husband's needs and her obligation to him. If there is one basic assumption I believe that most married women make, it is that their husbands are to serve them, and that any demands husbands make are insensitive and selfish. When I tell women callers that they are *obligated* to their husbands for such-and-such, I generally get two reactions: The first is surprise, the second is anger over perceived oppression.

Think about it for even one minute: How many women's mags talk about women's obligations to their men and children? Not many. The typical article is about deserving freedom: Day care vs. child rearing, sex out of wedlock vs. marriage, affairs vs. fidelity, and solo parenting vs. two-parent homes are offered as entitlements for women.

These days, so many young women are products of divorces or never created homes, were neglected by career mothers, were indoctrinated by the anti-family feminists throughout their schooling, and are surrounded by a culture that glorifies selfish gratification over sacrifice, it's no wonder so many of them are "surprised" to not only hear of their obligations to husbands and children, but are also amazed at the gratification derived from doing so. It is for them that this book becomes so necessary.

Many women allow themselves to take on the shackles of obligations to all sorts of family members and friends without at all expressing feelings of being oppressed or angry. Many wives allow destructive friends and relatives to visit or move into their homes against the wishes of their husbands, because these wives have decided this good deed must be done, and then—big surprise—they have no time for their husbands.

One caller, Karen, took this to the nth degree. She's been married six years and has an almost two-year-old son. Soon after she got pregnant, her mother was diagnosed with cancer and moved in with them. When the child was born, the mother's health really started declining and Karen considered herself responsible for taking care of both her mother and her child. She figured, I guess, that her husband could just fend for himself.

Then, one day, she caught him looking at some Internet porn and decided it was time to dump him. She took her son and her mother and moved in with her older sisters so they all could take care of Mom. After her mother died, Karen continued living with her sisters. Two years passed, at which point her husband expressed remorse and regret for having looked at some porn and wanted to get his family back together. Karen expressed her love for him, and while she believes that it is in the best interest of the child to have Dad in the home, the problem is, her husband's job as a vice-principal is in California, but she's back East with her sisters and wants to stay there.

DR. LAURA: But here's the constant, constant problem with you, Karen: It's all about you—your baby, your mother, where you want to be, how you feel. It doesn't seem to ever be about the fact that you're somebody's wife.

KAREN: Right.

DR. LAURA: I'm surprised you're agreeing. However, that is not the attitude of a married woman. It is getting so typical of women to assume that once they get married, they can be all self-consumed and he's just supposed to stand there and take it. Why is that?

KAREN: I don't know.

DR. LAURA: You need to move to where your husband is; he's supporting the family. Isn't that obvious to you? I guess not.

KAREN: Well, he says he is willing to come here and find a job.

DR. LAURA: He has a job. I can't believe you would demand that he give up security for the insecurity of trying to find a job. It's about time you actually left your family. When you got married, you supposedly formed a new one. You had unmarried, unencumbered older sisters around, medical support, hospice help, but you took this all on yourself and abandoned your husband.

What if it had been the other way around? What if all he paid attention to was the child, his mother, and his family, and where he wanted to be living and how he felt and how exhausted he was and how frustrated he was . . . and he completely ignored you? You would be feeling like there was no point for you; that you had no place in his life.

KAREN: Right. That's how he feels.

DR. LAURA: Where did you get this mind-set that made this okay?

KAREN: I don't know.

Actually, she did know—but somehow didn't realize it until I probed. It turns out that there are no men in her family at all—no father, no husbands for the older sisters, no men involved with the family the whole time she was growing up. Her mother and sisters were all divorced. Since men were never an issue, her husband wasn't an issue . . . until now.

DR. LAURA: Well, you know what? I'll bet they're all miserable and have serious emotional problems.

KAREN: Yes, that's right.

DR. LAURA: Do you want to be one of them? Or do you want to be a happily married woman with a child flourishing in the middle of that?

KAREN: Yes, I certainly want to be a happily married woman.

DR. LAURA: Then go be with your husband and make him feel important. Call him up today. Tell him you

love him and need him and that your child needs
him. Tell him you're coming.

Karen went on to explain that her main problem was that
she felt so obligated to her family, she didn't know how to get
out of it. I reminded her that when one is married, the spouse
and children go to the top of the obligation list. I also told her
I thought her family was "sick" because not one of them could
maintain a functional relationship with a man and they were
perfectly content to undermine hers.

At that point, her eyes were opened.

The truth is, there are only so many hours in a day and
only so much we can put our energies into. We have to make
choices. And if you don't pick you husband as #1, that favor
will, sadly, be returned.

Chapter 3

"YOU'RE A NAG!"

"Honey, it is part of your job as my wife to remind me of any duties I am not fulfilling, just as it is my job as a husband to remind you of your duties. You know I try my best, but if I don't know what I'm not doing, how can I do it, much less do it right? There is a difference between complaining and informing, between criticizing and reminding."

BILL

"So my suggestion for your book on the care and feeding of husbands? The number one thing I want from my woman is to stop complaining. It's easy to moan about how hard your life it. When I do catch my wife in a 'willing mood,' I first have to endure twenty minutes of her complaining about this, that, and the other thing before I get to touch her. I figure if I help around the house to take some of the burden off of her, I would win her affection. Wrong. It is never enough and I am always wrong. A little kindness would go a long way toward making the marriage better."

BRUCE

Bruce is right on. The universal complaint of men who e-mailed my Web site with their opinions about "The Proper Care and Feeding of Husbands" was that their wives criticize, complain, nag, rarely compliment or express appreciation, are difficult to satisfy, and basically are not as nice to them as they'd be to a stranger ringing their doorbell at three A.M.! These are not men who hate their wives or who were divorced; on the contrary, they are guys who love their wives and are trying to do whatever they can to please them. However, they are miserable and lonely.

Ken, another listener, is a thirty-eight-year-old husband of nine years with two children under the age of three. He wrote to express his opinion about a wife's nagging, explaining that it's not that a wife can never have a negative opinion or a problem with her husband, but that she should state the problem or concern without "bitching, fussing, arguing, guilt-tripping, or whining." Ken believes that a wife should say what is on her mind, discuss the possibility of a solution, and then move on.

I agree. The fact is that men don't like when women just "bitch about stuff," Ken said. In fact, they hate it. If a man can't find peace in his own home, where he should be able to feel relaxed, accepted, loved, and content, he begins to not only hate coming home, but he begins to hate his life. That sad reality is often the precipitator of stupid behaviors like drinking or taking drugs, Internet shenanigans, and inappropriate flirting or worse.

And it's not just issues of domestic disappointment that women nag or complain about; women can also be quite negative, hostile, and demeaning about simple "guy stuff." John and Maria wrote to me about their observations of couples stuck in just that hole. They described wives making fun of guys when they start discussing military issues, sports, or stocks. They wrote, "This same group of females would be livid if the guys made fun of their needlepoint, cooking, spa activities, or shopping tendencies." How true.

John and Maria also wrote about the wives they knew who have joined various all-female clubs and activity groups, who expect their husbands to be home to take care of the kids (which the husbands are glad to do) when they pursue these activities, but go crazy when their husbands want to do all-guy things without them, like fishing or playing poker or even going alone into the garage to hammer and saw stuff. Somehow the husband is seen as neglectful, insensitive, and selfish while the wife was just doing what she was entitled to do because she does so much for the family and needs some time to herself. Talk about insensitive and selfish!

Beyond the issue of complaining about "male stuff" is complaining about his romantic history. These are the calls that really test my patience. Just the other day on my radio program, a wife called to find out if she should confront her husband about a Christmas card he had received from an ex-girlfriend. It seems that this ex (one from a *long* time ago) sent an annual Christmas card, complete with pictures of her happy family and one of those "update letters." My caller was complaining about the personal stuff she shared and how it was so inappropriate.

DR. LAURA: What in the letter was provocatively, seductively inappropriate? And remember, you get one chance to prove your point, so give me the most egregious example, okay?

CALLER: She wrote about surviving breast cancer.

DR. LAURA: You are threatened and angry about a happily married woman who contacts your husband only once a year and only with a Christmas card and who has had breast cancer? Yikes, woman, do you often complain to him about such petty issues that are completely out of his control?

Believe it or not, she was stubborn about how inappropriate she thought this was and how she was going to confront him about it. I frankly felt very bad for her poor husband, who probably won't have a very Merry Christmas.

All of this nagging, nitpicking, and criticizing that men routinely get from their wives (be honest, girls, this is what we do) does not do much for their egos, which in turn results in them trying harder—for a while—and then giving up . . . and then we have more to complain about. Talk about a vicious cycle!

Jim, a listener, described himself as having a master of science degree and working at a college where he teaches a computer course to undergraduates, assists in teaching computer courses to graduate students, helps fellow faculty members with their computer problems, maintains a small research-and-teaching computer lab, operates equipment (dump trucks, tractors, chainsaws, etc.), and advises a student club.

> *"I have always had superlative evaluations on my performance. AT HOME I CAN'T DO ANYTHING RIGHT! I sometimes spend several minutes in thought on a task at hand, trying to decide exactly what to do. After weighing the pros and cons, I make a decision and act. Almost invariably I get, 'What did you do that for? Now I can't . . . ,' or I hear, 'Who put the ??? here?' or sometimes I get a straight-out 'That's stupid.'*
>
> *Many times my wife weighs in on a narrowly defeated second or third option while trashing whatever I had selected. Explanations are not wanted, and if I point out that I have just been called stupid, an argument is more likely than an apology.*
>
> *It is something that wears you down like erosion."*

He means it. And Cathy's husband also meant it—just before he left her. Cathy, another listener, wrote to me of marrying when she was, according to her, "twenty-five and very immature." She admitted being caught up in herself, her home, and her children. Her husband would walk through the door after a hard day of work and all she would do was complain about the kids and the house. She would nag and complain about *her* life, which was, in reality, very privileged. Her husband never got a hug from her. She never sat down and really asked him how his job was or how his day went or if he was happy.

> *"I tossed aside his feelings and I, in the end, lost my husband to another woman and my children lost their father. God, if only I had been as nurturing to him as I was to my children. I am now in my late forties and I could kick myself for my selfishness and stupidity. Boy, have I ever learned from my mistake."*

Cathy remarried and treats her current husband quite differently. She always asks him how his day went, has him describe to her the details of what he's doing, and looks as interested as she can even when she doesn't follow or understand what he's talking about. She wakes up with him and brings him coffee before work and a glass of wine when he gets home—and no jumping on him with house or personal problems the minute he walks through the door. Such simple gestures. Such a difference in her home.

I'm convinced that too many wives don't know what to do or how to communicate if they're not complaining, nagging, or criticizing. Many times on my radio program I have suggested to women that they approach this problem as they would a new puppy. I tell them that instead of constantly screaming "NO!" to every little annoyance, transgression, or difference of perspective, opinion, or style, they should compliment the heck out of the things they like and want. Betcha that way you'll get more of it!

Clarence, a listener, wrote that his wife is very much like

the little girl with the curl right in the middle of her forehead: When she is good, she is very, very good, but when she is bad, she is horrid . . . and abusive.

In order to raise five kids in the country (where his wife wishes to live), he commutes and works a total of thirteen hours a day. Although he's exhausted when he comes home, he always tries to find something that needs doing and would make his wife's life easier . . . and perhaps make her the good girl. He often washes the dishes, and when the drainer becomes full, he dries them.

> *"I would appreciate even a quiet 'Thank you,' but I get, instead, a 'YOU KNOW YOU SPREAD GERMS WHEN YOU DRY DISHES WITH THE DISH TOWEL!' So next time I stop when the drainer is full and work on something else. Response? 'WHY CAN'T YOU DO ALL THE DISHES?' So next time I carefully stack dishes three feet high. Response? 'YOU KNOW THAT I GREASED THE BREAD PAN AND I WAS PLANNING ON USING IT AGAIN, AND NOW THANKS TO YOU CAUSING ME MORE WORK, I HAVE TO GREASE IT ALL OVER AGAIN!'*
>
> *So the next time when I can no longer stack any higher, I wait a couple of hours for the dishes to air-dry and put the first batch away. Response? 'ONE OF THE SPOONS WAS STILL DAMP WHEN YOU PUT IT IN THE DRAWER!' So next time I leave the dishes and spend two hours cleaning the living room. Response? 'WHY DON'T YOU EVER DO ANYTHING AROUND THE HOUSE? CAN'T YOU SEE THE DISHES NEED TO BE DONE?'*
>
> *So next time I stand in front of the kitchen sink with tears running down my face, wanting to help out with something that will be noticed but petrified that I will discover one more way to*

do the dishes wrong. Response? 'I WANT A DIVORCE. I
HAVE TO DO EVERYTHING MYSELF ANYWAY!'
  I would be much happier with a quiet 'Thank you.'"

When discussing this issue of nagging with my husband,
who suggested that I had the necessary expertise to write this
chapter (was that a hint?), he said that he just figured that nagging was part of the female XX chromosomal information—
that it was simply built into the DNA. But even if that were
true, would it let us off the hook? Can we say we wives are
entitled to nag because it's our genetic destiny?

I think not.

But I believe it is more typically female and that women
almost believe it is their birthright and that men would be lost
without it.

I think not.

Rachel, a listener, wrote that she also thought nagging was
an inherent right of wifehood. Although she and her husband
had been married for only about a year, they were arguing
every day! She wanted the two of them to go into marriage
counseling to help him discover what he was doing wrong.
She felt that all her needs were important. For example, she
would nag him about how to soak dishes, or get angry at him
for forgetting something he'd said in passing three months earlier.

  "I had to exercise my right to complain or he wouldn't know
  when he would be doing things that bothered me. And he, being
  my husband, was not supposed to get mad—just take it like a
  man."

More like a doormat, she really means. Obviously, this
caused problems in their relationship. She finally admitted that
she was to blame, and that meant that she had the answer to

the problem: She simply buttoned her lip. A miracle occurred. They argued less. Their marriage got better. She told him she was sorry for causing him so much grief.

She concluded her letter with, "Which brings me to the point: Complaining is not a virtue. Complaining does not lead to anything good."

No, but appreciation does lead to something good. Examine these two scenarios and then tell yourself which you think will get the desired results:

The garbage needs to be taken out.

Scenario 1: Yell at him every five minutes to remind him that the garbage has to be taken out. Then berate him for not having done it yet in spite of your reminders and in spite of whatever else he might be doing. Then start escalating things by bringing up everything else he's done to annoy you in the past decade. Then, once he's finally taken the garbage out, tell him, "It's about time!" Then storm off to your room, pout, and turn your back to him in bed.

Scenario 2: Let him know you've wrapped up the trash and that it's sitting by the back door, and ask him if, when he has time, he would please dump it in the trash bin. Don't bring it up again (why bother, because the trashman isn't coming till morning, anyway?). Catch him just as he's coming back from tossing the bag in the can. Give him a big kiss and tell him that it was a big help because it's hard for you to hold the can lid up with one arm and pitch a very heavy bag with the other hand.

Which approach do you think will ensure that the trash is out of your kitchen every night like clockwork?

Jo, the listener who suggested Scenario 2, wrote:

> *"Men are doers; simple, straight-line types. The reason they have a tendency to rescue damsels in distress is because of their need to be admired for their chivalry."*

Men love to hear, "My hero!" What makes it so difficult for their wives to give them that accolade? Where does so much false pride, ego, resentment, and stubbornness come from?

Charlie, a farmer, wrote about a conversation his wife told him she'd had with a neighbor of theirs. Evidently, Charlie's wife admitted complaining to this woman that Charlie was not willing to do the chores around the house that she wanted him to do, how and when she wanted them done. The other woman told Charlie's wife that she didn't have the same problem with her husband because she "rewards him" for doing the household chores that she would like him to do.

After his wife finished the story, she said to Charlie, "I hope you don't expect a reward for doing the household chores." Charlie proceeded to get his hat and was starting for the front door when his wife asked where he was going.

He told her he was simply going to see if his wife's friend needed her lawn mowed.

"My wife still doesn't get it. I would be much more willing to do the chores she wants me to do if I got some show of appreciation for doing them."

How shortsighted of Charlie's wife. It does seem that many woman see "schmoozing" their men as an example of their being "controlled." Sarah, a caller, and I tussled over this point.

Sarah and her husband have been married fifteen years. She described marrying him because he was so nice. I immediately came back with the suggestion that she made that choice because it put her in control. Now she sees his being "nice" as "weak," and is frustrated with his lack of helpfulness in disciplining the children.

SARAH: We talked about it and I told him that what I wanted from him is to help me.

DR. LAURA: Except he never does it right, right?

SARAH: It's not that he doesn't do it right. It's that he doesn't do anything at all.

DR. LAURA: Because when he does it you criticize him. Whenever he tries something, in your eyes it is inadequate. So now he just doesn't get involved. This is a vicious cycle. I suggest you both go into counseling. The counselor will remind you to hush up and back off and only suggest something to him. He has to move forward on his own and not complain about not having control when he refuses to take it—albeit under the difficult circumstances of you not being willing to either give up control or share it. If he wants to be held in respect in your eyes and the children's eyes, he is going to have to be more aggressive, which is not naturally his nature. He can't blame this all on you, either! Now, I want you to watch yourself all week and observe yourself criticizing when he does exert control. When you do that, he figures, why bother.

SARAH: Right, that is exactly right.

DR. LAURA: So even if he only does whatever sixty percent of the time or sixty percent of how you'd like it, it's better than zero. You see, Sarah, it seems wonderful to be in control, but eventually you become overwhelmed and need help and want a partner. For example, if Johnny intentionally threw the water into the shrub, go to your husband and say, "Can you please deal with that?" and then walk out of the room. Don't even watch it happen. And then—this is the most important part—say, "Thank you."

SARAH: Okay.

It is very difficult for men when they come home from work only to hear how they're not doing enough around the house. When they help with the dishes and only hear about how they didn't do the laundry, they begin to feel like failures. One listener, Chris, had gone through this for so long that he eventually had an affair with a woman who, obviously, treated him more like a hero. Eventually, filled with remorse and love for his family, he ended the affair and has worked with his wife to repair their marriage. He concluded his letter with these important words of wisdom:

> "If I had to summarize, I'd say, 'Please, ladies, recognize that we men do love you, and although you may not think we do much around the house, we do the ugly stuff like change the oil and mow the lawn and get up early when it snows to shovel a path to your car and start the car so it will be warm when you get in. We would walk through fire for you to get you a quart of cookie-dough ice cream in the middle of the night, because we love you.'"

Roy, a listener who describes himself as married but lonely, believes he is trying to be a good husband, but that it's hard to be good when the feedback is mostly related to the times he doesn't meet his wife's expectations. He longs to be her hero, but she evidently prefers to point out that he leaves the lights on, doesn't dust everywhere he should, misses spots when he's washing the dishes, interrupts her when she's talking, chooses to drive the wrong way in the parking lot, drives too slowly . . . and so on.

He gave this advice to women:

> "If you can't accentuate the positive, at least acknowledge it. The world is full of messages to men that there are standards we don't meet. There is always another man who is more handsome, more virile, or more athletic than we are. None of that matters if the most important person in our life looks up to us, accepts us as we are, and loves us even though we aren't perfect.

Maybe there is a part of the small boy that never leaves the grown man, I don't know. All I know is that the husband who has a wife who supports him and praises him for the positive things he does is the envy of all the other men who have to live with criticism, sarcasm, and constant reminders of their failures."

Ouch.

All of this criticism of men does not make them feel *more* loving, and it also makes the complaining wife feel less love for her husband. That's true; the very act of criticism destroys warm feelings toward the target of that criticism. But on the other hand, the simple elimination or diminution of criticism adds to loving feelings.

Sara wrote that she never realized that she was nicer to telemarketers than she was to her husband, and that many of her married friends would also treat total strangers nicer than their husbands. She never could see the good in anything her husband did—she could only see the mud that he tracked into the house.

She wrote that she couldn't quite remember why or when she started to change. Maybe it was simply that all the negativity became too unbearable for her. Or maybe it was when she realized that she could not have been too happy when she would leave the house without wearing makeup or dressing nicely, or when she would slob around the house in sweats and tees.

"Over time I have adopted ways to make my husband feel like my champion because he is, and for a long time I would go out of my way to belittle him and his significance in life. I have yet to find out really why I was that way, but life is wonderful now and my changes have come back to me ten-fold. I love my husband more and more each day."

I often get calls from women who complain about losing that lovin' feeling. They, of course, imagine it's because something is missing from their guy. Turns out that more often than not, though, they've been stomping on their own loving feelings with their mistreatment of their men. Imagine that.

I am often struck by the pettiness of the complaining, and by the complete inability to see another way of handling a situation. Too often the negative perception that seems to always pop up first ends up dominating all emotion and reason.

Tina called me about her marriage of about one year. This was her second marriage and she and her husband had a newborn baby. Now, I give you that at least for the first year after birth, and especially if the mother is actually raising her own child, emotions can get a bit edgy. But this was ridiculous.

She angrily told me that her husband had lied to her about losing his wedding ring.

TINA: He states that he lost his wedding ring over a month ago. He didn't talk to me about it. He proceeded to go to the jewelry store and purchase another, identical ring. I found out by the jewelry bill coming in the mail. It turns out that he found his ring and now he has two rings and a jewelry bill and has lied to his wife.

DR. LAURA: Lied to his wife about what?

TINA: He never told me that he lost the ring.

DR. LAURA: Why is that a lie?

TINA: Because I feel like he should have talked to me.

DR. LAURA: Wondering why he didn't come to you is not the same as him being a liar. He didn't lie. Noticing how you get, I can understand why he didn't want to say anything to you. You seem pretty volatile. So he went out and replaced it before you would find out and get mad. He didn't want you to be hurt, or worried, or angry. He was trying to solve the problem and keep you happy. So you call a radio program and want to hang him.

TINA: I really feel like he was dishonest. . . .

DR. LAURA: You know, Tina, your *feelings* aren't facts, and your *feelings* ought not be weapons.

TINA: So you think he did the right thing?

DR. LAURA: Yes. It was one of a few "right things." It certainly indicates his wanting to not hurt or upset you. And it also appears to indicate that he didn't think he could talk to you about it without you getting angry.

TINA: (sarcastically) I am sure he will be glad to hear that.

DR. LAURA: You know, Tina, I hope you will start treating him a little better, because you have a newborn and you are already down one marriage. I think you should not have your fangs out so quickly.

TINA: Okay. That's reasonable. I guess they are out quickly because dishonesty is a sore point with me.

DR. LAURA: Well, it wasn't dishonest; it was desperate. You are exaggerating everything now because you have some bad memories. You could destroy today.

TINA: I don't want to do that.

DR. LAURA: Well then, when he comes home, I want you to put your arms around him and say you know you were real off base. Tell him how nice it was of him to try to save the day and replace the ring so you wouldn't be upset. Tell him you just got carried away. Don't mention the past. Say "I'm sorry," and it will all be smoothed over.

TINA: I appreciate that and I will do that. I value your opinion.

Obviously, one reason the fangs may come out quickly is that many women, who have cycled through too many intimate relationships, shack-ups, and marriages, have developed a well of pain and disappointment. They don't want to be hurt . . . again. They become hypersensitive and take quick leaps into misassumptions.

Wives need to love their husbands as though they've never been hurt before. Otherwise, they destroy today.

Unfortunately, it's hard for many women to find support for that healthy point of view from their women friends, relatives, or even "help" groups.

Wendi, a listener, wrote to me that during the fourth year of her tumultuous marriage, her husband suggested that she participate in their church's Wednesday-morning "Moms Group." Once she'd done so, her husband noticed changes in her on Wednesday evenings, but they weren't the good ones they'd both hoped for.

> "The women's group was not the help I'd been hoping for. Instead of finding practical ways to become a better mother, the group was a gripe session for women to vent about their husbands' idiosyncrasies, bad attitudes, and failures in general and in specific. I was becoming trained to complain and whine about real or imagined behavior and look for sympathy from other women. I discontinued participation. My husband and I sought real counsel from a godly couple, our pastor and his wife of over fifty years. They taught us to respect one another, our family, and our privacy. It was important for both of us to be fed from the same trough so that we could work together."

Grace, another listener, was bolder in her reaction to the "bitching about husbands" that can go on in groups. In her letter she described being with a group of women from the restaurant at which she worked. It seems things started slowly, with women complaining about how their men didn't wine and dine them since their marriage, but then it snowballed into a ferocious male-bashing session.

Grace herself was having marital troubles and her home life was shaky. After about an hour of everyone airing their grievances, someone noticed that Grace hadn't said anything yet. They offered her the platform, acknowledging that she must have some really great complaints. It may have been at that point that Grace had her "revelation." She proceeded to tell the group what she thought.

> *"Most of their complaints were their own faults. They were shocked. I asked them when was the last time they cooked their husbands a dinner and ate it by candlelight on the porch? When was the last time they gave their husbands a back rub? What I was asking was when was the last time they did something for their husbands. All the women just stood there and looked at me.*
>
> *I believe that the give-and-take in a marriage gets forgotten by women. Somehow we feel that once we are married, our part of 'give' is doing dishes, cooking dinner, and watching the kids. We then expect our husbands to reward us for this with back rubs, flowers, dates—but we don't give these things in return.*
>
> *Do we reward him for going to work, mowing the lawn, fixing the cars? He needs to be rewarded for these things, too. But that's not why you should do these things. They are not reward points. You do this because you love him.*
>
> *If you want to keep a fire in your marriage, you need more than the spark—you need to add fuel. So if a woman starts the spark, the man will follow and add some kindling, then she can add more and soon you will have a happy marriage."*

How did so many women get to this unhappy place of not understanding how truly "simple" men are in their requirements and how much benevolent power their wives have over them? Why did notions like assuaging "male ego" and using "feminine wiles" rocket into disrepute? How is it that so many women are angry with men in general yet expect to have a happy life married to one of them?

There are a number of reasons for this, and I believe they all revolve around the assault upon, and virtual collapse of, the values of religious morality, modesty, fidelity, chastity, respect for life, and a commitment to family and child rearing.

With a religious foundation, both women and men appreciate that they become more complete when bonded to the opposite sex in holy matrimony. Without it, though, women may see marriage as either an option equivalent to the usually temporary arrangement of shacking up, or as the threat of oppression, or as an impediment to the fulfillment of some important material goals.

When modesty, chastity, and fidelity were in vogue, women who valued themselves as more than sexual objects or outlets were respected by society in general and men in particular. Now women have to contend with men taught to expect sexual favors as a part of casual dating. As a result, women ignore their true nature to bond, and find themselves getting more and more hurt and bitter as they search for meaning in a culture telling them meaning has no meaning.

When there was awe and respect for life, an "accidental pregnancy" was met with commitment and responsibility because women expected it and men were accountable. Now men expect an accidental pregnancy to result in an abortion because society has trained them to see this as a temporary inconvenience, or they expect to walk away because they've been told men aren't needed to raise babies.

Commitment to marriage and child rearing was once viewed as the pinnacle of adulthood identity, so that women looked carefully for the "right" man for the job, and parents were consulted for opinions and blessings. Now, with so few sustained marriages and children growing up with complex family trees made up of multiple marriages, divorces, and out-of-wedlock children, fewer women look upon marriage and child rearing as stable or even normal.

The feminist double whammy of the elevation of women without men (and children without fathers) and the dismissal of men as unnecessary or even dangerous has certainly not contributed to the kind of positive disposition that women need in order to function well within a monogamous, hetero-sexual, committed relationship.

This grandiose self-centeredness about the value of women, paired with a virtual disdain for men, leads women to treat men badly. Too many women look at men with a sense of entitle-ment versus an opportunity for selflessness. Why? All of those forces taken together have given women a false sense of superi-ority.

Combine this false sense of superiority with the element of not being properly psychologically fed by their fathers and you have a recipe for tension. Women have a hunger for being protected and cared for—whether they want to admit it or not. This hunger is amplified when there was no father in the home. The man or men who then enter their lives become mixed up in their psychological need to replace Dad. This makes for inappropriate expectations about what a man can and should do, which get in the way of a healthy, two-way relationship. While there is always some wonderful mommying and daddying going on in all marital relationships, the com-pulsion to always give or receive such is a serious problem, as their partner is either force-fed or starved. That lack of balance destroys relationships and corrodes people's psyches.

Sara wrote about her experience with the attitude of enti-tlement:

> *"I was under the impression, when I was first married, that a husband was supposed to be controlled and bend to the wife's whim. Everyone said men were stupid and they needed to be*

educated and trained. I was becoming more and more frustrated because my husband wasn't bending. I'd demand he act like a 'man,' but failed to treat him like one. I was so concerned about what I deserved that I almost lost sight of the fact that he deserved something, too. I took advantage of his love for me and misinterpreted it as weakness.

As I matured and grew spiritually and emotionally, I realized that it was my actions that made him react the way he did. I now give my husband the respect that he deserves not only as a husband and a partner, but as a human being. He has in turn become the 'man' I never allowed him to be . . . and is wonderful at it. I know that this is one of the most important life lessons I have learned."

Louise, another listener, e-mailed me concerning her understanding of the dynamics of her original family, which clouded her perception of men and marriage. Her father had been violent and mean-spirited. Her response was to fear and hate him. While she wanted to have a happy, loving, well-adjusted family of her own, she was too mucked up in worrying about being "the victim" that her mother herself portrayed. With therapy, Louise came to realize that her mother was not a victim at all, but someone responsible for her own choices, actions, and behaviors. Her mother was hateful toward men, seeing them as spoiled children who must be managed, and she raised her daughters to see life in that same light. "My father was the perfect match for her," Louise recounted. "He bullied her, but she controlled him by allowing herself to be the martyr—the superior person."

Louise came to realize that for her to have a successful marriage, she had to take responsibility for her choice in a mate, and how she would treat him. When she first married, naturally things were difficult because it was hard to *not* put into practice what she had learned in her original family. But now she says, "I am so grateful for my family, and I am proud that we treat each other with kindness, respect, and patience. In short, we nurture our relationship with each other, not our neuroses."

Many of the wives reading this book may feel stuck in some inexplicably angry place. Perhaps this story, told by Louise's minister, will help:

A grandfather was talking to his grandson. "Grandson," he said, "there are two wolves living in my heart and they are at war with each other. One is vicious and cruel, the other is wise and kind."

"Grandfather," said the alarmed grandson, "which one will win?"

"The one I feed," said the grandfather.

That is precisely why I steer women who are troubled in their marriages away from women's groups, where men-bashing is a cross between entertainment and denial of personal responsibility; I steer these women away from the run-of-the-mill feminist-oriented psychotherapists, for whom a happy relationship with a man is simply not necessary; I steer these women away from griping and gossiping with their girlfriends about their annoyances with their husbands. The reason I do all this serious steering-away is explained in the minister's story: The more you dwell on the negative, the farther away you get from appreciation of the positive, as well as the motivation to contribute in a more healthy way yourself!

One small step toward a wife's taking responsibility is to keep lips buttoned over things that *do not really matter.* I'm fond of repeating a phrase sent to me by a retired Marine master sergeant: "Is this the hill you wish to die on?" Frankly, asking myself that question always makes my priorities instantly fall into place and reduces my tension about whatever it is I was worked up about.

Wives need to remind themselves that when their husbands

do something differently from how they would do it themselves, it does not constitute a breach of sanity or a display of contempt. It is merely a *different* way to do something. Instead of immediately correcting a husband, first see if there is something you could learn (could happen, you know?), then see if the job gets done (that was the goal, wasn't it?), and then offer a compliment (you like those, too, don't you?).

One husband, "L," wrote that wives should not "micromanage."

> *"Trust your husband. Recognize that he has his own ways of doing things. They don't have to be done your way to be adequately done. If the toilet ends up clean, it doesn't matter if he didn't give it your 'special touch.' If he has the kids for the day so you can attend a baby shower, don't leave a huge list of detailed instructions. As long as the two of you share the same rules and values, you should trust him to create his own relationship and 'caring style' with his children without your intervention."*

When women micromanage, their husbands give up trying to please them, and then the wives complain that their men don't do anything for them. Wives need to look to the mirror for the typical source of that problem.

Essentially, micromanaging is about controlling. That issue of control makes men feel that they are ultimately not the men their wives wished they'd married. Bill, a listener, shared the example of his first wife (obviously not his last wife) buying him a pair of jeans. He'd carefully written down the size, brand, and color he wanted. He even told her the store with the best price. She came home with Dockers—khaki, the wrong size, and clearly the wrong type. He thanked her for her efforts, explained the inadvertent error she'd made, and asked her to please exchange them for what he wanted. She agreed, and returned from her next shopping trip with another pair of Dockers, not jeans, in yet a different color.

> *"This time she explained that she did not like the way I looked in jeans, and that what I needed, and all I was going to get, was a pair of Dockers. It turns out what she really wanted was a different guy to fill the Dockers. She spent twenty-five years trying to make me somebody else. Know who your husband is and accept him. He is what he is. She clearly knew what kind of guy I was before we married. She just assumed she could nag, lie, cry, manipulate, and scream at me till I became someone else."*

He did become someone else: her ex-husband.

This nonacceptance of who your man is can get even uglier. What horrifies me time and time again is the evil some wives perpetrate in the name of their "feelings." This is an extension of the entitlement issue. And the two expressed "feelings" that can bring almost any husband to his knees are "hurt" and "uncomfortable." I have had innumerable arguments with wives on my radio programs over their over- and misuse of those feelings, which is often tantamount to cruelty or evil in their attempt to control and dictate.

The more typical scenarios seem to occur in stepfamily situations. I'm amazed at how many women marry men with prior marriages and children and expect all of that to disappear when they come on the scene, as though his earlier life had evaporated into the Twilight Zone.

And the men suffer horribly. Brian was one of those husbands.

BRIAN: I'm presently married for three years and have two children, two and three. I have an ex-wife who lives out of state, with whom I have an eight-year-old son. My ex-wife is now divorced again. I don't get to see my son often because of the distance and other factors.

DR. LAURA: Oh dear, that poor little boy has suffered a lot of loss.

BRIAN: Yes, I'd hoped her marriage would work so he would have a male role model.

DR. LAURA: How can I help you?

BRIAN: My question is: I'm supposed to have him for the whole summer. I've never had him that long before, but now his mom is under stress and is willing to let me have him. But my wife is uncomfortable with that.

DR. LAURA: Well, uncomfortable. . . . So what? Everyone is going to be uncomfortable simply because it's new and different. So? Talk about the issues, find ways to deal with them.

BRIAN: Here's my question for you, Dr. Laura. Would it be inappropriate morally to tell my ex-wife that it's just not possible to have him for the whole summer?

DR. LAURA: You're just not going to have me go there, sir. You made him and virtually abandoned him. He's your son, you need to raise him.

BRIAN: I agree with that completely. But my wife says she does not want to have him there for the whole summer. She said she can't do it.

It was at this point that I was ashamed for my gender. Of course I see the strain in raising two small children under the age of three. What I don't like to hear, but hear too often, is women not wanting their stepchildren around because there will be no children before theirs! How disgusting! Even more disgusting is how resentful wives can get about their husband's time, affection, and financial resources being directed at his own children. There is so little sensitivity to the fact that he already has those bonds and that they matter, and that his responsibility to any children he's had is a moral imperative.

What I told Brian, as I tell the many husbands who call with this type of question, is that he needs to *inform* his wife that the boy is coming for the summer. Period. Any difficulties in scheduling, transportation, and activities can be worked out.

BRIAN: And if she says no?
DR. LAURA: There is no "no." You say, "Honey, you married a man with a child. There is no 'no,' there's only 'how.'"
BRIAN: So—no matter what?
DR. LAURA: You're his dad. Period.

I suggested he also watch out for how many times and in how many ways his wife tries to manipulate him by telling him she's "uncomfortable," as though that were a stop sign. Obligations and responsibilities are usually not discomfort-free zones. That's part of what makes rising to those occasions such an extraordinary measure of character and love.

We all think we'd like to be able to control everything and everyone around us. We imagine we'd be safe and secure— always on familiar turf. Frankly, the texture of life does not come from the familiar (which is comfortable), but from challenging ourselves with the unfamiliar.

Tonya, a listener who termed herself a "control freak," got this lesson and shared it with me:

"I take my husband for granted. I know this, as I have recently become an avid listener of your program and have learned from hearing some callers who sound just like me. I am a control freak and I am always trying to dominate my husband. It mostly has to do with our financial health. Somehow I see that

in trying to control his spending, etc., what I am really doing is punishing him. I also like feeling superior to him in this area— that somehow I am better than him as the queen of the check- book. Just because I don't think he really needs a sander doesn't mean he shouldn't have it. He probably doesn't really think I need all of those candles and Pampered Chef products either . . . but he must be punished for his past mistakes! I'm going to read your book, and I'm sure it will help me find other ways to show him that he is appreciated. And, as I have heard you say so many times, if he feels loved and appreciated, those feelings will most likely be reciprocated."

You can bet on it.

However, the problem is often getting the wife to see, to acknowledge, to accept, to realize that she is, in fact, control- ling. While many women are quick to the draw to aim at some extraneous word or deed of their husband's as evidence of his being controlling, it seems that some are blinded to the reality of their own actions.

Crystal, a caller, was one of those women. She'd read my book *Ten Stupid Things Couples Do to Mess Up Their Relationships* and was focused on the chapter whose title she remembered as "Stupid 'Control.'"

DR. LAURA: Actually, it's "Stupid Power."

CRYSTAL: Stupid power. That is my husband and I know I can't change him. I was wondering what I could do to let him know that this isn't going to work.

DR. LAURA: Give me an example of what he does— some behavior you wish would change.

CRYSTAL: Okay. We had an argument. I apologized— actually, I left him a message at his work. When we got home and we were talking, I asked him how his day was. He said he was really busy. I asked him if he got my message. He said that he had but that he is in a really busy, difficult time at work. I walked away. Then I said that it really hurt my feelings that he didn't even acknowledge my apology.

DR. LAURA: Okay. This was your example of his being controlling? I don't see any controlling except by you. Your husband has to—now listen carefully, Crystal—behave in a certain way or you pull out your big gun. And you know what your big gun is? "You hurt my feelings!" He just told you repeatedly that he had a busy and difficult day. None of that mattered to you at all, did it? What mattered to you was a certain response that you wanted at the time you wanted it. Crystal, my love, in your scenario, you are the controller.

CRYSTAL: Really?

Really.

Now, I don't want to give the impression that all controlling of husbands by their wives is a bad thing. To the contrary. It just depends on what's in your heart, the intent in your mind, and the actions of your arms and lips. Pamela's letter was right on target with this issue. She described a conversation she'd had with her husband some fifteen years into their marriage. He'd been loud and clear about the fact that the main reason his first two marriages had ended was that his ex-wives had tried to control him. Pamela smiled sweetly and informed him that she'd been controlling him for fifteen years. He smiled back and said that he knew that she'd been "playing him," but that he liked the way she did—and why.

"1. He knew I loved him unconditionally: He was diagnosed with congestive heart failure six years ago. 2. I like him: He's my best friend. 3. I respect him. 4. I make sure that his needs are met both physically and emotionally: He's a very passionate

Hispanic guy. 5. I make him smile. In return for these things, he showers me with love, respect, kindness, jewelry, anything I want. Recently, I told him that I wanted to quit my job as an executive to start my own consulting business. He didn't bat an eye—because he knew that it would make me happy."

Controlling and giving are opposites, and giving is a more powerful tool than controlling to get what you want as a wife. Moreover, what a wife gets back from giving is offered with enthusiasm and love, not fear or resentment.

Mary Ann, a listener, acknowledged to herself that she was a controlling, moody, nagging wife. Her husband's response was typical: He pulled away and wasn't very loving. Once the marriage seemed to be falling apart, she went to a (good) therapist who helped her understand that the only thing she was really in control of was herself, and she needed to work on herself first before her relationship was going to work.

"I did exactly that and started treating my husband with respect instead of control. I did the loving things that wives are supposed to do for their husbands—cooked his favorite dinners often for him, rubbed his back, let him do his 'guy' things without me and without my complaining about it, stopped nagging about what he wasn't doing and complimented him when he did do things right.

Believe it or not, he started treating me how I had always wanted to be treated as a wife. My advice is that if you continue to nag, control, and be an unpleasant person to be around, then your husband is not going to want to be around you or treat you how you want to be treated. If you love, respect, and treat him how you would like to be treated, he will begin to return the treatment back to you."

Now, I can just hear some wives annoyed that this book is aimed at them. "After all," I'm sure they're saying, "don't men have any responsibility? Why is it on our backs to change for them? Where is her book on 'The Proper Care and Feeding of Wives?' Hummf!"

No, I probably will not be writing about the care and feeding of wives. Why? Because the truth is that when it comes to home and relationships, women rule. This is a book about how to rule wisely and lovingly. If a woman does not marry a sociopath or narcissist, then she's got her basic "male package." And your basic male is a decent creature with simple desires: to be his wife's hero, to be his wife's dream lover, to be the protector and provider for his family, to be respected, admired, and appreciated. Men live to make their women happy.

The cruelest thing a wife can do to a husband is to never be happy. And don't forget, being happy is more an attitude than a reality. When things are going bad, when there are problems and challenges, disappointments and disasters, it is obvious that happiness is going to be undermined. However, when one looks for that little peek-hole in the sky where the sun *does* shine through, then it *is* a lovely day.

And it becomes a lovely day for everyone you touch. As Christine, another listener, wrote:

> *"I also make the effort to pick up the toys, comb my hair, take off the paint-spit-up-yogurt-stained shirt I'd been wearing since six A.M. A little sweet-smelling body spray, lip gloss, some mouthwash, and I'm ready to welcome him home with a big kiss. Some days it's more of an effort than others, but my husband does not want to go anywhere else but to his loving home each evening."*

Chapter 4

MEN HAVE FEELINGS? REALLY?
YOU'RE KIDDING!

"Over time, much if not all attention has been placed on men being sensitive and understanding toward women. This has been a good thing. As a man it has taught me well. I am a much better listener. The drawback is that wives believe they have little responsibility to also consider how their husbands feel. I would like the same thing out of my wife that I have been taught to give to her: equal treatment and acknowledgment of my feelings."

CHRIS

"This I am proud of as a wife: I have never, ever said anything hateful to him—even in the heat of anger. Whatever we might argue about will pass, but hurtful words stay FOREVER!"

KAREN

If Karen were in the majority, there would be no need to write this book. However, my experiences in private practice (as a Marriage and Family Therapist), on air, and with the e-mails, faxes, and letters I've gotten from my listeners draw an alarmingly clear picture of, in my opinion, gender abuse. That abuse consists of an amazingly crass disdain of wives for husbands' feelings. And it causes husbands deep pain.

John, one of my listeners, responded to my on-air request for men's input on the subject of the Proper Care and Feeding of Husbands by pointing out the pain men feel, which can drive them to stupid behaviors, such as having affairs.

> *"My experience tells me that since men seem to be afflicted with prurient thoughts about sex about seven times a day, the right hussy with the right words and the right moment and . . . need I say more? Having known several males who have had affairs, I think several things are important to know.*
>
> *While I have known happy men who have had one-night stands (and all regretted it later), I have never known a happy man who initiated or was involved in an affair. Affairs start and are fueled by something missing in the marriage—and it generally isn't sex! The affairs that I have known about started with a man alone, crying on a park bench or into an 'adult beverage.' A man in tears usually isn't alone long."*

John continued by noting that the men he has known over the last two decades who have had affairs had been telegraphing their unhappiness for years before they just gave up. Their complaints fall on deaf ears. Then come the affairs. Then come the wife's tears about how *she's* been wronged and *her* feelings are hurt.

While this scenario is not at the root of all affairs, it is definitely common. Whenever I've talked to a man after he's had an affair and ask him, "Why?" he usually first says, "I don't know," which shifts later into, "It's about how she [the honey] made me *feel* about myself."

The obvious issue here is that, frankly, men are generally not all that forthcoming about their feelings, at least not in the way we wives are. As women, we're used to the tears, the desire to talk endlessly about "what happened," the constant assessment of our emotional status, the way we describe things in terms of how they *make* us feel, and, of course, the way we have hurt feelings as a result of just about anything anybody does.

Nope, men are generally not leading with their feelings. They generally don't walk through the door after work with a burning need to talk about what feelings might have gotten tweaked that day. They'll more likely talk about a challenge they've faced, or will have to face. Because they don't cry all of the time, or have to call their mothers or best friends to go over emotional issues a thousand times like their wives do, wives make the mistake in thinking that they don't have feelings.

Oh, puhlease, don't tell me wives can't notice hurt in their eyes, stress in their stooped posture, pain in their silence, fear in their hyperactivity, anger in their tenseness. Or do wives immediately translate their husbands' pain into annoyance that their men are being selfish or insensitive?

Danette, a listener, communicated just that truth. She related a story about the time she was sitting with her best girlfriend, chatting. It was this dialogue that woke her up to the realization that she had never paid much attention to how she was treating her husband. She had asked her friend a question, and ended the question by remarking that she hoped her friend didn't mind her asking—that she wasn't offending her or hurting her feelings with the question. Her friend said, "Nothing you do will ever offend or bother me. But my husband regularly bothers and offends me." Danette, although realizing her friend was half jesting, realized that she was also half serious.

She then got to thinking about her own husband and how he had a tendency to frequently get on her nerves. She started wondering why that was. Later that week she got into one of her typical arguments with her husband, complete with defensive, nasty jabs. It dawned on her at that point that she probably got on his nerves, too.

> *"Then, like a slap in the face, it hit me: I was taking advantage of him without considering his feelings. I always considered my girlfriend's feelings because I didn't want to offend her, or make her mad, or lose her friendship. How stupid is that? I didn't have the same consideration for my own husband! It's like I wasn't caring about what he thought or felt."*

I always admire people who are willing to look in the mirror, hold themselves accountable, have remorse for the things they've done wrong, and have the willingness to repair and not repeat their unpleasant actions. That is exactly what I hope all wives will do after reading this book. And if wives can't easily slip out of their self-centered mode ("It's all about my feelings"), perhaps they can at least try to consider that the perspective presented here could give them more of what they want. The main source of husbands' bad attitudes, negative responses, and disappointing behaviors is their wives' attitude toward them and *their* feelings. Plain and simple.

I've even started warning men who are engaged and calling me about some issue with their fiancées' family or the wedding that how they're being treated now, whether or not their feelings or opinions are being considered, will only get more so when they marry. Generally, they just can't believe it. They think that their fiancées' bad, insensitive, selfish behavior is only due to all the stress involved with making wedding plans, and that when folks throw the rice, it will get all better. No way.

J.A., a forty-year-old unmarried woman, wrote to me about her girlfriends' horrible behaviors with their fiancés while planning the wedding. She describes their insensitivity to the feelings of the men:

"It seems that as soon as the ring (and, of course, size does count in this department) is on their finger, women stop responding to their men in a positive, affectionate, respectful way. During the planning of the wedding, men's opinions are, for the most part, completely disregarded. Then the women begin 'complaining' about their fiancés. The women believe their men are there to satisfy every whim."

A call from Jeff, twenty-seven years old and about to wed in two weeks, provides a perfect example of this problem that many wives-to-be have in not taking into account the feelings of their men. Weddings are not just about the one wearing the lace.

JEFF: Basically, we have a full house. Two people on my side RSVPed late, and as a result, my future mother-in-law would like for us to uninvite them based on the space issue.

DR. LAURA: Is it the space issue or the money issue? You can always stick two more chairs and two more plates at a table.

JEFF: We resolved the money issue.

DR. LAURA: Then tell dear mother-in-law that you're not going to uninvite people important to you.

JEFF: Well, I did that, and now my fiancée is all upset about it because it now has become a control issue as to whether or not I will tell my mom that they can't go.

DR. LAURA: This is a control issue between you and your girlfriend—not you and her mother. Maybe you need to step back and see what you might be getting yourself into. If your girlfriend's mother is this controlling and insensitive, and your girlfriend is defensive on the side of her mother, you, frankly, are screwed. And I wouldn't give five cents for your mind in five years. If your girlfriend is already showing disrespect for your feelings and disrespect for the people who mean something to you, I imagine that after the wedding she is not going to show any more respect for either.

JEFF: I see.

I sure hope he does, because men like Chad probably didn't and are now paying the price.

Chad and Sherrie called my program about their conflict. They've been married for three years, and he adopted her two children, ages ten and nine. The current problem was about Sherrie's constant, lengthy visits to her parents' home.

CHAD: My wife has just returned to Springfield, Missouri, where we live with the girls, after spending five days with her family. She now wants and is planning to go back to Iowa for the state fair. She plans on being gone for ten days and we've been arguing over this a little bit, I guess. I believe that being gone for ten days after being gone for five days is pretty excessive. My first pick would be for her to be here and maybe just take a weekend or a four-day weekend up there versus being up there for ten days.

DR. LAURA: Sherrie, do you want to give me your twenty-two cents?

SHERRIE: Yeah. Well, all my family live up there in Iowa. I am a very family-oriented person. I have been with these people my whole life, and it has been hard for me being away from them and moving to a state where I don't know anybody. So, therefore, I try to go up as much as possible.

At this point in the conversation, I asked Chad to hang up the phone and not listen to the radio so he wouldn't hear what I was going to say to Sherrie. I knew I was going to let her "have it," and thought she'd be more likely to take in what I had to say if she wasn't embarrassed by his hearing it.

DR. LAURA: What is in your mind, woman? You got a guy to marry you and adopt your two kids, and you have the nerve to tell him that your family orientation is directed toward your mommy and daddy? This is very foolish. Your husband is your family. He adopted your kids and made them his family. For you to keep running home to Mama is telling him that he is secondary after all he's done for you. You are out of your mind to hurt him this way.

SHERRIE: So the girls shouldn't ever see their grandparents?

DR. LAURA: You can always let them fly to Grandma's and let them stay for weeks while you stay around home and have intimate time with your husband. Don't be making him feel like he is disposable for weeks on end. I don't think you understand what he's done for you.

SHERRIE: Yeah, I do. I'm very grateful.

DR. LAURA: Well, you're not acting like it.

SHERRIE: So I shouldn't go for ten days?

I couldn't believe that after all I said, she came back to herself.

DR. LAURA: Only if you're planning on being divorced sometime soon. I don't understand you. You are so lucky. How many thirty-something women with two kids can get a decent guy to take care of them? You need to not treat that cavalierly.

She never got to the point of actually acknowledging showing him respect or being sensitive to his feelings. Her husband probably falls into the "Stupid Chivalry" chapter of my book *Ten Stupid Things Men Do to Mess Up Their Lives.* In this chapter I describe how men, needing to feel important and valiant, often get into situations that can best be described as "saving a damsel in distress." They believe that if they save her, then she will fulfill their needs and dreams, but in most cases they just end up with a distressed damsel. In this case, Sherrie's feelings are at the center of her universe, and Chad is in an emotional black hole.

Chad was demonstrating his *feelings* of love and his *feelings* of need and his hurt *feelings* of neglect and abandonment by telling her to stay home—with him. What about that display of *feelings* wasn't clear? Should he have cried, screamed, and banged things? Should he have gotten drunk and smacked her? Would these be feelings she could recognize? Certainly, but then he'd be called a rude, insensitive, boorish, violent brute.

And this is the pickle juice in which many a married man marinates.

Brian, a listener, expressed this very annoyance. He gave these four examples to describe his wife's utter disregard for his feelings and her ability to turn it all around on him:

1. When his wife wants to go do something with her friends, she says he should trust her and allow her that freedom. When he feels that he needs some alone or buddy time, she says that he doesn't love her or want to spend time with her—even when she's invited! It's all about her feelings—not his.
2. When she spends money, it's okay because it's something she "needed," and she should have the freedom to spend money when she wants to buy something. When he wants to spend money, she calls him irresponsible. It's all about her feelings—not his.
3. They see her family about twice a week. When he

wants to see his family, she complains that he's not being sensitive to her feelings about her family. It's all about her feelings—not his.

4. "Basically," he writes, "it's her priorities that matter. She'll have the whole weekend planned, while I'd love to have some downtime together. She'll say that I'm not supporting her." It's all about her feelings—not his.

So let's take this time to get to husbands' feelings. Jim, a listener, writes:

"Despite our rugged outward appearance, most men tend to have delicate psyches. I know four very happily married men. In each case their wives make a point of stroking their egos and making them feel *that they approve of them. Consequently, these men practically worship their wives."*

But how can husbands *feel* respected, appreciated, or loved when they are the constant brunt of their wives' negativity about everything?

Melissa, a listener, wrote to me about an incident that occurred during her first year of marriage. She and her husband were at another couple's house for dinner. The wife started complaining about her husband and Melissa started to do the same thing about her husband. What she didn't realize was that although her husband was in another room, he overheard everything.

That night when they were snuggled up in bed, he called her on it and told her that it had really hurt him to hear her talk like that about him. Chagrined, she apologized profusely and made it a point from that moment on to smother her husband with compliments whenever she was with a group of women who were "bagging" on their husbands.

"As much as men's bellies need to be filled with delicious home-cooked meals," she wrote, "their egos need to be filled with 'yummy food' as well. I have found that if I speak blessings about my husband, then blessings are what I get in return."

I believe that women in general have been taught to disdain the "male ego," ascribing to it a sense of phoniness, immaturity, and weakness. Ladies, what makes the male ego issue any different from our "body ego" issue? Our husbands have to tell us our bodies (thighs, hips, and butts in particular) are perfect and that these pants don't make us look fat because (a) we don't want to hear the truth, (b) we can't handle the truth, and/or (c) if they tell us the truth, then we're hurt, they're mean and insensitive, and the relationship is shot down in mid-flight.

We, as women, want to know that we are lovely and desirable *in general* because of our shapes. They, as men, want to know that they are desirable by *us* because of their prowess in providing for their families, satisfying their women sexually, and having the strength and leadership to confront challenges and protect their families and values. They *need* that and they need that from us.

A wife can tear down a husband's necessary sense of strength and importance more easily with a look or a comment than can torture in a prison camp. Surviving the latter *is* a demonstration of a man's strength. Men don't easily survive the former: Their wives' approval is as important as oxygen; surviving their wives' lack of approval is emasculation.

By her own description, Eva was one of the emasculating wives. She wrote that after she and her husband had kids, their marriage felt more like two people who only happened to take care of the kids together, and less like a husband and wife living life together. She had lots of resentment about how her husband "didn't understand her" and "didn't do things right to help her feel happy and satisfied."

This all changed when she finally recognized that "my husband was a person with goals and desires, frustrations and needs, all his own. While I felt he didn't understand me, I didn't understand him, or see him at all, except for what was wrong."

Far from being oppressed in their marriages, most wives are the oppressors. I can hardly remember more than a handful of times while I was in private practice working with couples in troubled marriages that a wife would respond with openness, compassion, and sensitivity to her husband's display of feelings. The typical response would be shock, anger, reproach, threats, and tears. That's oppression, folks.

Thankfully for her husband, Eve was one of the handful:

"One night, after my complaining about something, he opened up and spilled out a lot of things I'd never heard before. For the first time I saw the strain of stress from work, fathering, husbanding, home-owning, etcetera, and how overworked and overtired and overwhelmed he felt. It was a bitter and cynical monologue, and I previously would have been very hurt and angry with him—but for some reason this time I was shocked by the depth of his emotion.

I thought not of me and my reaction to his words, but of how his attitude got there in the first place and how helpless and horrible he was feeling. I truly felt empathy and concern for him and his situation."

In the ensuing days, Eve continued to listen without defensiveness, and made suggestions to her husband in an attempt to be helpful. She prodded him to get back into golf even though she'd virtually ripped that from his life because she'd always felt that (1) if he loved her, he'd want to be with her, (2) he needed to do things around the house and with the kids, and (3) she needed a break. She admitted never even considering that maybe he needed a break, too.

This was the beginning of seeing him in a good light and treating him with much more respect for his feelings.

> *"Now, several years later, we both are much more caring about each other, and willing to see the other's needs and point of view. Funny, as I changed, my husband didn't seem so bad. Did he become more pleasant in response to my more pleasant attitude, or was he really not all that bad to begin with?"*

Both.

It's worth reviewing the issue of a husband's feelings and the male ego to point out how vital a wife is to the well-being of her husband. This list of basic points supporting that concept is culled from enumerable e-mails from husbands:

- A man needs to feel strong and needed as a protector for women—basically, to conquer the beast and rescue the fair maiden.

- What every man wants is for his woman to make him feel that he is strong and the head of the household. I am not talking caveman-style, dragging the woman around by her hair, but just as the leader of the family.

- A man wants respect, kindness, and love from his woman.

- A man wants to be put on a pedestal, not so that he can look down on everyone, but to show him that he is the most important thing to his woman.

- A man needs his woman to show him that she needs his strength to help her through life.

- The man should be the major breadwinner in the family. Every man needs a battle or war to win to prove to himself that he is strong and capable of conquering any and all dragons that life throws his way. Taking care of his family by working and providing are his battles.

- A man needs enthusiastic approval, appreciation, and respect from his wife for being a competent man, husband, and father.

- A man needs his wife to show some interest in his interests, especially when it's an activity she may not "get" or like. Just being there is important.

- A man needs his wife to greet him after work with love and enthusiasm.

- A man needs his wife to care about the day he's had.

- A man needs to know that his wife is sexually satisfied by him.

- A man needs his wife's encouragement in order to be a man.

Some of the hostile input I initially received from women when setting out to write this book concerned their disgust at the notion of men's "feelings," which were perceived as "neediness." And, of course, if a husband has hurt feelings or is needy, then the spotlight is off the wife and she's then required to care-take. It's a bit disgusting that so many women were so up front about not "feeling" that they want to or should have to do that for their men. Yet their expectations about their husbands' solicitousness were resolute and infinite.

The fact is, men probably are more emotionally needy for feedback from their wives than wives are from their husbands. Women turn to their mothers, their friends, their neighbors, their coworkers, their relatives, their shrinks, their hairdressers, their manicurists, and most media to get validation—earned or not. Because of this willingness to gossip and solicit support from the far corners of their personal universes, women in general rely less on their husbands' approval. Which, of course, explains part of why they don't care enough about their husbands' feelings, or fail to pursue those feelings as an issue.

Men don't gossip; they are more private. By and large, they tend to get a sense of approval from their success at work and from their wives' happiness. That makes us wives more accountable for their well-being than we may like to be. So, talking to a grown man, the father of your children and the major financial supporter of your family, in that "mother tone," as though he were a naughty or irresponsible child, is in direct opposition to his wanting to have a wife and family who are in awe of him for who he is and what he does for them.

As John, a listener, wrote:

> *"Nothing discourages a man more from trying to be a good husband than the feeling that no matter what he does, his wife won't be pleased with him. Sadly, I know many men who feel that way. I am grateful to be with a wife who believes in and appreciates me. The more she tells me how much she loves and respects me, the more I want to do nice things to honor her, and the better I feel about myself. Everybody wins!"*

Lloyd, another listener, contributed this analysis about men and their feelings:

> *"Men, whether husbands or bachelors, do not share their thoughts and feelings as readily as women. We do not see any need to bother others with our feelings. We just deal with them. If something needs to be done, we do it. If something needs to be said, we say it.*
>
> *Many times we just don't want to deal with the consequences of saying what we feel out loud. We don't want to*

explain ourselves. So we just live with our thoughts and adjust. Wives must find ways to encourage their husbands to share feelings by allowing them to do so without consequences. Husbands should be encouraged to share their feelings without being accused of being insensitive and stupid. Let us talk. Be supportive. Permit us to have opinions, feelings, and thoughts that do not agree with yours."

The majority of men who wrote to me and commented on the issue of their expressing feelings made that same point. Ken wrote:

"Frequently, when I get angry over something she has said or done and have the temerity to express my feelings, she just dismisses it as me being overtired, or some other trite toss-off. This is akin to a guy seeing a woman angry and saying, 'Guess it's that time of the month again!' "

Other men wrote that when they'd tried to vent about something, their wives would somehow find a way to make it their fault! That goes for everything from their wanting more sex to saying that the lawn mower was broken.

The stereotype of a woman insensitive to a man's feelings is, unfortunately, well-earned. There isn't a day on my radio program when I don't struggle with some wife or girlfriend over this issue. Here are the synopses of several calls that demonstrate the severe magnitude of this problem for men. I am quoting them, with annotation, in some detail, because they clarify the main problems involved in women treating their men's feelings with disrespect or disregard.

This first call has to do with misplaced loyalties the wife has for her original family. Danielle has been married for ten years and has four children. The central point of tension is that Danielle and her sister have always been "best friends." She

describes her husband and sister as both having strong opinions and personalities. Her sister and her sister's daughter
(note: no husband there!) come to visit Danielle's mom, who
lives nearby, for months on end, and her niece then comes
over all the time to play with Danielle's children. Somehow
that seems to give her sister permission to pop over whenever
she pleases, which is a problem because she doesn't get along
well with Danielle's husband.

DR. LAURA: If they are oil and water and they don't get
along, you need to minimize the overlap.

DANIELLE: I understand.

DR. LAURA: And, frankly, if there is a choice to be made,
it's obviously got to be your husband. He is the father
of your four children. You don't want to make him
feel secondary to your relationship with your sister. If
your sister can't come over and be nice to your husband for the sake of your marriage, then she is not a
very good best friend. Maybe you need to sit down
with your sister and tell her that when she comes to
your house, no arguing—just to be nice because you
want family serenity.

DANIELLE: Well, he isn't very nice to her sometimes.

DR. LAURA: I wonder if she didn't just earn that. It is
his home and maybe you are not showing enough
respect for that. What is the ongoing problem he has
with her?

This is when the story got even more interesting. The niece
was over almost every day for weeks or months. Danielle and
her husband have certain rules about behavior—normal
stuff—and it turned out that the sister confronted Danielle's
husband because he attempted to (reasonably and responsibly)
exert discipline in his home.

DR. LAURA: How outrageous of your sister to make your
  home a day-care center for her kid and then, instead
  of showing eternal gratitude, come over and get in
  your husband's face with complaints! And you don't
  throw her out?

At this point in the discussion, Danielle started to laugh—
somewhat out of nervousness, but mostly, I believe, out of an
awareness that she'd been caught doing exactly what she knew
was wrong: She was intimidated by her sister, desperate for her
friendship, and mindless about the destructive impact of her
lack of defense on her and her husband's family.

DANIELLE: I knew you would say that. . . . It isn't funny.
DR. LAURA: No, it isn't. You have a marriage you don't
  respect. You think it's funny that you cater to your sister over your own husband? How can you expect to
  stay married with that kind of attitude, or doesn't it
  matter?
DANIELLE: It does.
DR. LAURA: Then act like it.

This scenario of caring more for the feelings of friends and
family than for those of husbands is not an unusual one.
Women seem to imagine that their husbands can, will, and
ought to take a lot of abuse and keep on ticking!
  This next call has to do with many women's hypersensitivity to being "controlled"—even by a husband's feelings.
Valerie's call, while not unusual, was a whopper. Instead of
choosing a friend or relative over her husband, she'd picked a
cat! The issue could have been severe allergies (which is more
typical in these cases), but in Valerie's case, the cat was down-
right hostile toward her husband, hissing and attacking. I was
so stunned that I responded with pure sarcasm.

VALERIE: I know it sounds crazy, because who would pick a cat over a husband, but I'm having issues with this where I feel like I don't want to have to get rid of the cat. And I don't know what to do.

DR. LAURA: Well, you've already found the solution—just let your husband feel miserable and feel like he doesn't matter. I think that is the really smart way to go. That is the best way to keep a man really lovingly tied in—sarcasm free of charge.

VALERIE: I know—and I know that is probably how he is feeling, because I just got off the phone with him and he said so.

DR. LAURA: But we wives know that what husbands feel doesn't really matter—it is only what we need, what we want. Listen, I have read all the feminist stuff. Men are just oppressors and he is obviously just trying to control you. He is a real bastard about this. What you have to do to teach him a lesson is buy more cats.

VALERIE: I know. And, you know, that is probably what my friends would say.

DR. LAURA: Men are supposed to just go along with what pleases us no matter what they have to suffer, right? He has no right to have these feelings or make these demands or want to be comfortable or want you to make a choice between him and an animal. Right? He has no right. He is just a male.

VALERIE: No . . . he is more than that.

DR. LAURA: How would he know that from you?

VALERIE: (laughing) I know, and I know that's how he's feeling. And I feel just the way you've described. I'm wondering why he is being such a wimp about a hissing cat. So what? She isn't biting him.

There it was: What was emotionally upsetting to him (a hissing cat and a wife having to debate the cat vs. him) was being trivialized. I asked her how she dared trivialize his feelings and then expected him to give a damn about hers.

I saw two options. Either she was superficial, spoiled, and a complete twit, or there was a more significant issue to exhume. I guessed the latter, and I guessed right.

DR. LAURA: Tell me about the part of you where his being hurt or upset really doesn't matter.

VALERIE: Well, I guess because I don't want to be controlled. Yeah, I guess I don't want to feel like I am being told to do something, so now I have to do it regardless of whether I like it or not.

DR. LAURA: Okay. Do you think your husband should feel controlled when you want something?

VALERIE: No.

DR. LAURA: Oh, Valerie, that is so not true. But the trick you do in your mind is this: You don't call it control when you want something. You call that a reasonable request, which should be granted if he loves you. But when he does the exact same thing, it's control. And you know that is true because you are worried about your girlfriends telling you that you have become an oppressed female. You come from a man-hating environment.

VALERIE: True.

I ended the call by telling her that she needed a healthier set of friends and a healthier mind-set about the give-and-take in a relationship. And she needed to find a good home for the recalcitrant cat.

This next call focuses on the issue of wives wanting to control everybody else to create the perfect picture that makes them feel more comfortable. Gina's husband's parents were divorced when he was two years old. Evidently, her husband and his father had never developed any bond or closeness.

GINA: My question is whether or not it is morally right for me to not include my father-in-law in his grand-children's lives. My husband is against this and very upset.

DR. LAURA: Why would you undermine your marriage to have this "father-in-law" involved with your kids? Why would it be more important to have this distant stranger involved with your kids than it would be to keep your marriage strong?

Astonishingly, she denied she was aiming her gun in that direction. Our discussion pointed out that she knew she was making her husband annoyed and angry, but didn't give thought to that. "So what, he's angry," is the unbelievable attitude so many women express when they're designing life the way they want it, rather than helping their husbands cope with the truth of the way it is.

GINA: A broken marriage is not what I want.

DR. LAURA: Then you have to stop pushing this issue, no matter your rationale for doing so in the first place.

Here it comes!

GINA: So . . . what is important is how *he* feels toward his father?

Bingo! A breakthrough! Or so I thought . . .

GINA: Should he at some point be man enough—

DR. LAURA: Oh, my gosh. I don't believe this. You don't even think your husband is a man because he has made this choice to disengage from his absent, neg-lectful sperm donor?

GINA: I guess this is the picture-perfect thing that I want. I just don't like confrontation.

DR. LAURA: Well, if you were woman enough, you would handle it. How does that shoe feel on your foot?

GINA: It feels like an ouch, but I can take it.

The next call involves what I call the "world is only on my shoulders" syndrome. Anna is a stay-at-home mom with four children ranging from fifteen months to eleven years.

ANNA: Lately, I have been feeling angry and resentful at my husband. He is a really great guy. He works a lot of hours and the night shift so I can be at home. I feel that he is just someone else that needs something else from me.

DR. LAURA: Anna, do you remember your wedding day?

ANNA: Yes.

DR. LAURA: Aside from the pretty dress and all the presents, do you remember your vows? What were they?

ANNA: To love and honor.

DR. LAURA: Were those vows amended with caveats that you don't have to love or honor if you're tired or annoyed?

ANNA: No.

DR. LAURA: Do you want to stay married?

ANNA: Yes.

DR. LAURA: Then you have to make your husband feel that he is coming home to a woman who considers his feelings and needs important. He has to come home to a woman who rewards him for all he does for his family.

ANNA: It just seems that we are only polite lately—and with the new baby, it is really hard.

DR. LAURA: Yes, it is . . . no question about that. And it is

really hard to work two shifts and come home to a
distressed wife and four children desiring his attention and love. It's five for him to deal with, too, you
know. And, truth be told, you do need some R&R
and reward for your day. I'll tell you how to get that:
When he walks through that door, give him hugs and
kisses and a chocolate brownie if he has a sweet
tooth. Tell him how much you appreciate the fact
that he has been out all night busting his butt so that
you could stay home with the kids. Watch what this
tired man will perk up and do for you. . . . *ANY-
THING YOU WANT!* That includes sex, a great
relaxer, a foot rub, a bubble bath, playing with the
kids—anything. You know I'm right.

ANNA: Yes, thank you.

This next call has to do with disagreements in raising and
disciplining children. Chris's husband did not think that their
fifteen-year-old daughter should go out to a football game on
the evening we spoke, because she goes out a lot. The irony
was that Chris had given the daughter permission to go, in
contradiction to her husband's decision, even though Chris
agreed that the girl was out way too much.

I noted that they were actually not in disagreement. I suggested that perhaps they ought to make these decisions together,
in private, before presenting the decision as a team.

CHRIS: I guess that the only problem is that quite often
we disagree, and when we do, he says I am not supporting him and he says it is like the kids and I are
against him all the time.

DR. LAURA: Perhaps he's actually right! Maybe you are
protecting "your little girl" and giving her everything
she wants and by doing that you are bypassing your
obligation to respect his opinion and decisions.

CHRIS: And that is a bad thing?

DR. LAURA: Yes, because the first and foremost relationship in that house is between you and your husband. And this is what your daughter will remember when she makes decisions in her marriage. If she sees you disdainful of a man, she'll likely do that, too. In addition, being this spoiled, she'll have lots of troubles in life when she doesn't automatically get her own way. The social life of teenagers has to be moderated.

CHRIS: Right. I agree with that.

DR. LAURA: Then if you agree with that, you don't always disagree with him after all. I think you need to be more honest about how you are always the "good guy" with your daughter and perhaps all the other children, too.

CHRIS: Now you're sounding like him.

DR. LAURA: Well, it is true. You are doing that. You are focused on "being liked" by your kids, rather than being a parental partner with your husband in raising those children. Now start working with him. He will be blown away that you actually gave a damn about his opinion.

CHRIS: He will. He will be really blown away!

It is of life-and-death (to the marriage) importance that a wife and mother not make her husband feel as though the children are sufficient for her fulfillment. One caller, with her husband on the line, made that very claim. I couldn't believe she could be so blindly cruel to him and expect him to still be there for her in any size, shape, or form—which, believe it or not, was the reason she called: to complain that he didn't do enough for her! One woman, after hearing this call, wrote to me:

"Initially I was shocked that she would say this in front of him, and let's be honest here—in front of you, too! But as I got

real with myself, I realized that what was so shocking was that I have said things that are just as hurtful to my husband. You really hit home with me when you said that behaving this way is cruel and abusive. I wanted to cry.

You also pointed out to the caller that she need not be concerned with her husband behaving in a more loving, attentive manner toward her. Instead, you said, she should concentrate on providing him the love and affection and position of importance he deserves, and that he (since men are 'not as complex as women') will automatically return it to her.

I was frightened as you talked about men leaving their wives for other women who make them feel good about themselves. As you talked to this woman about how difficult it would be to raise her children without this father who provides for the family and loves them, I realized that I never want to be in that situation.

Thank you, Dr. Laura, for opening my eyes to my own selfishness, self-centeredness, and destructive behavior. On this Valentine's Day, I am committing to doing what is right for my relationship with my husband: to nurture him and our marriage with the same energy I put toward nurturing my daughter."

While it is true that men's feelings are not neon fixtures on their person the way women's are, that doesn't mean they don't have feelings. Women, you don't have to see them to know that they are there. Just think. Think about things from their perspective—as though you were in a mini-camera behind their eyes. Imagine his whole day, his challenges, problems, threats, difficulties, frustrations, fears, and exhaustion. You know he has feelings about all of that.

Think about what confronts him at home. You know he has feelings about all of that. Everyone, anyone does.

It's just a matter of thinking about somebody outside oneself. Wives must accept and allow their husbands to have the same feelings, cares, and concerns that they have. Assume it. Don't badger your husbands for female-like expression of feelings—just assume it, and behave accordingly, with understanding, compassion, and support.

I have told innumerable women this. I have asked them to imagine what any human being would feel at the end of the day or at the end of an ordeal. He doesn't have to lay it all out in order for a wife to be sensitive and caring. Men don't need to air out the bitter details of their day. They simply need loving support and reassurance.

The saddest story I received was from a physician. On one particular day, he had performed a cardiac operation on a child. Later, problems developed and he was committed to a prolonged two-hour intense resuscitation effort . . . that was ultimately unsuccessful. The mother of the child, consumed by grief, physically attacked him and attempted to choke him to death.

> "This, even to a physician, is a severe loss and emotional stress. Upon my arrival at home, the anger at my missing the scheduled time to get ready to go out that evening was apparent and my explanation that the child had arrested was met with, 'I'm sorry, but can we go now?'
>
> The expanded facts were never discussed and my responses to a disaster were never considered. I tried to tell her that things were awful, but her response was, 'Well, we have been waiting, so let's go now and I don't want to hear any excuses.'
>
> Needless to say, fewer incidents were shared. My summary statement is: REMEMBER YOUR HUSBAND IS ALSO A HUMAN BEING WITH THE SAME EMOTIONAL NEEDS THAT YOU HAVE. TREAT HIM HUMANELY."

While this story is dramatic, including as it does the death of a child, no matter what the job, husbands come home with stories and reactions. Does anyone at home care?

In conclusion, Bill, a listener, wrote:

"Being married for the second time, to a woman the opposite of my first wife, I am painfully aware of the significance of the Proper Care and Feeding of Husbands.

I know in my heart that my wife loves me by the way she treats me; by the way she looks at me and looks after me and my children. She listens to me about my work, my problems, my dreams, and gives feedback when I ask. I know in my heart that she cares about all of my being.

I would walk through fire for my wife. I FEEL that she loves me. More than anything, I want to make her happy because of all the love and caring and feeding she gives to me. I give back to her from the bottom of my heart, and it is the best feeling I've ever had in my life.

Your question, Dr. Laura, is what do men want from their wives? For me it is to FEEL in my heart that someone truly cares for me and loves me; that I am immensely important to her. I can only get this through my wife's actions. Words are a whisper, but what she does for me is a thunder."

Enough said.

Chapter 5

"HUH? HONEY, WHAT DID YOU SAY? WHAT DID THAT MEAN?"

"Women are disappointed in the man who doesn't read her thoughts. I think that realizing that a man is just that, a man, is the most impossible thing a woman can do. They are different creatures. They think differently, they feel differently, and they communicate differently . . . and they're NOT WRONG for that. They are beautiful, too, in their own garage-grease, fix-it, thinking way."

MARIE

"I used to intuitively expect my husband to be a woman, and felt constant frustration that he didn't think, feel, need, act, and communicate just like me. It took me a long time, discussions with my father, and some reading before I realized that he was simply going to be different and that I needed to accept and work with these differences."

CATHERINE

Catherine continued with the admonishment that younger women like herself, brainwashed into thinking that the sexes are the same to various degrees ("and other feminist gobbledygook"), had better wise up, wake up, and smell the coffee. She remarked that her life has been much better since she got a grip on what is reasonable to expect from a man.

That's a very important point. The bigger the difference between what one *expects* and what *is,* the greater the disappointment, hurt, and, usually, anger. It is therefore important to have realistic expectations. In the realm of husbands and wives, though, women do tend to have largely unreasonable and unrealistic expectations of their men. This happens when women don't accept or respect the unique masculine qualities and quirks of men.

Daniel, a listener who works for an electronics company, sent me an engineer's view of the difference between men and women. His contribution basically consists of a photograph of a rectangular control panel divided equally between the top and bottom parts. The top part has only one on/off toggle switch. The bottom part has some *forty* switches and dials, and *two* switches for on and off. Someone has labeled the upper part MEN and the lower part WOMEN, as a joke about how complex women are, with all those complicated, fine-tuning necessities, and how simple men are in contrast.

Marital communication would go much better if women would accept without rancor that men simply have different communication styles and imperatives. I realize that this sounds like I'm putting the burden of communication problems on women, but perhaps there are some good reasons to do so. Verbal communication is much more important to women, and essential to their being—and that, it appears, is all in the wiring.

The differences between men and women begin in the womb. At first, all fetuses' brains are virtually the same. At about nine weeks of gestation, though, testosterone surges through the male (XY) fetus, changing the direction of general development toward masculinity.

With respect to communication, the result of those differences are apparent early on in childhood. Studies in child development have documented behavioral differences in children even in the first year. In one study, a barrier was placed between the child and his or her mother. The boys, wanting to get back to Mommy, try to get around or over the barrier, or they try to knock it down. The male response is physical, and it's aimed at solving the problem. The female children, on the other hand, verbalized their distress, and their mommies came and picked them up. The female response is verbal.

As children grow up, parents notice that their daughters are unbelievably verbal and usually prone to high drama. These same parents notice that their sons are "men of few words" but lots of action. Obviously, within the populations of both men and women there is variation; nonetheless, these generalizations exist for a reason: They represent the larger population and reveal some focal points of problems between husbands and wives trying to communicate in a manner that enhances the husband and the wife as well as the marriage.

One of the most typical complaints I hear from wives about their husbands is that the men won't sit and talk about things. I'll ask, "What things?" The response usually is, "Things. Just things. Everything. Anything." I might then ask the wife why it is so important to her that he be able and willing to talk about . . . anything, and she will inevitably say, "Because this is how to be close . . . loving . . . intimate."

Men are more likely to perceive their wives as being close, loving, and intimate when the wives wear something revealing to bed, make them a sandwich with a beer, or suggest that they go play some rounds of golf with their buddies. Women are more likely to perceive their husbands as being close, loving, and intimate when the men do what they've been told or asked to do, give romantic gifts, or listen patiently—and without comment—for the nth time to the same emotional account of some old grievances with a friend, relative, or coworker.

The first thing I usually remind women who call complaining about the communication problems with their husbands is that the callers are probably not even communicating
but using their husbands as girlfriends or shrinks; the husbands
are supposed to show interest, agree, and remain uncritical and
unchallenging. Husbands imagine (so foolishly) that their
wives are telling them something they actually need to know
because they're supposed to do something about it. Otherwise,
the men can't imagine why the "communication" is happening at all. It confuses them, then frustrates them, and their
response is then to turn off. That's when they unfairly become
labeled insensitive.

Therefore, the major mistake wives make in communicating with their husbands is to imagine that their husbands are
supposed to be their best *girl*friends. Most women I remind of
this error get hostile, as though I'm taking away some entitle-
ment. I inform them that this is simply an erroneous expectation. When they don't want to accept that, I remind them that
their way isn't working—the proof is that there is too much
rancor and distance in their marriage—and maybe they ought
to try seeing what treating their husbands as *men* will bring
that's different from what they're seeing now.

John, a listener, can't seem to understand what women
don't seem to understand about men and communication:

> "I dated a woman for a few months, and whenever we drove
> anywhere, if there was a lull in the conversation, she would
> demand, 'What are you thinking?' 'I'm not thinking anything,
> dear.' That was never good enough, and she would spend the
> rest of the date sulking and planning her retribution against
> male domination—or something or other.
>
> I told her that men aren't bright enough to drive and think
> at the same time, and that just added more fuel to the fire.
>
> We look at the birds, we look at the trees, we look far

enough down the road to make sure someone doesn't plow through a red light and kill us all; but driving and plotting and manipulating at the same time takes far more hard drive than we were ever issued.

If a man tells you he isn't thinking anything, he probably isn't.

Can't see how that is so hard to understand."

Women, you'll be off track more often than not if you constantly imagine that your husband's quiet is a sign of trouble. He's probably not withholding something from you (unless you're a volatile pain in the butt when he does confide in you), and he's probably not simmering with some secret anguish (because men generally don't ruminate over feelings of hurt or disappointment) unless you notice him sleeping less and drinking more.

The truth is that wives generally overwhelm their husbands with communication. Much of what motivates that communication might better be dealt with through personal circumspection, triaged for significance, selected for true communication (connecting) value, whittled down to its essence, timed better, and expressed more appropriately.

Marla, a listener, admitted that she tended to tell her husband "everything."

"This often included how I felt about people, situations, weather, etcetera. I held back no emotion. From his perspective this was whining and complaining. I didn't see it that way. From my perspective I was just 'sharing my heart.' However, I started noticing that he seemed to want to talk less and less to me.

Years later he was brave enough to confront me and tell me what I was becoming. It was almost as if I were treating him as my dump. Like it was his job to take all the stuff I wanted off my chest.

Things have been so much happier in our home and our marriage since I've started taking my problems to God first and trying to deal with my own emotions before 'dumping' them on him. He's more than willing to hear when I have a problem now . . . because he isn't bombarded with them constantly."

I'm reminded of the theatrical production *Amadeus.* Mozart has just finished leading the orchestra in concert, playing one of his original pieces for the king. His archrival rushes forward and, in front of the king, proclaims that the work was fine but that there were "too many notes."

In Mozart's case it wasn't true; for many wives it is. Terri, one of my listeners, confirms this observation:

"I also believe that we as women talk too much in our conversations with our husbands. We say they never listen to us, but let's face it, we usually put in way too many details to keep them interested!

I mean, really, would you want to listen if they were telling you every detailed play that took place in a football game they'd seen? I certainly would be bored silly if my husband did that. He can tell me if his favorite team won and he can even tell me a great play that was in the game, but any more than that, I would for sure start to zone out.

If we cut down on the details and ask them more questions about their day (without pressure for answers, though), conversations would become more two-sided and more pleasant."

This is probably one of the most difficult concepts for wives to accept: that they should cut down on the communication as a way to improve it. Somehow, wives have come to believe that with respect to communication, more is better. Wrong. More appropriately selected and timed is better.

Cooper is one wife, and listener, who gets that point. She's been married four years and is a stay-at-home mom to a three-year-old daughter and one-year-old son. She says that she's learned to give her husband at least a half hour when he comes home from work before she bugs him about anything. During that decompression time, she doesn't ask him to talk about anything, doesn't volunteer anything about her day, and doesn't nag him about what he does with that "downtime."

In other words, she lets him unwind. Without that decompression he would be edgy the rest of the evening and unwilling to communicate. Now he is more chatty during dinner and evening activities. Now she can talk and question him about their respective days.

Cooper admits that it is still a struggle to fight against the urge to unload her whole day on him the second he gets home (as though *he* didn't have a "day," too), but that it is becoming easier and easier to wait a little longer for a welcoming set of ears.

Robert, a listener, has a wife who has also learned to temper her eruption of communication.

> *"When I am done with my personal time and come back upstairs, I am relaxed, and I am open to 'hear' what she is saying, and everyone is happier. She has also come up with a catchphrase. When she prepares to tell me something, she reminds me that she doesn't need anything fixed or solved— and that cues me that I'm just supposed to listen, which is what she really wants."*

Some of this caring behavior toward husbands comes from wisdom and practice; some of it comes from maturity. Natalie, a listener, realized that she had to learn how to take care of her own emotions better. She understood that, as a woman, she is more prone to emotions and emotional changes that her husband can't keep up with. "Sometimes I need to deal with my own feelings and not 'work them out' with him," she said. That's where the maturity comes in—realizing that, as a woman, we have responsibilities to our own well-being, and our husbands' sole purpose in life is not to tend to our mercurial moods. A husband's need not to be drowned in an onslaught of verbiage and emotion must be respected. Natalie continued:

> *"Once I thought through my feelings on my own, I could tell my husband how I felt, but I could be RATIONAL (imagine!) while doing it. I guess I basically started growing up emotionally and have pretty much stopped overreacting to situations, ideas, and apparent predicaments that came up . . . and simply react."*

And what makes wives think that communication has to be all verbal? An embrace, a warm look across a kitchen table, a smile, a kiss—these are all forms of communication, too! They aren't verbal, but they are powerful forms, which, like pictures, can be worth more than a thousand words.

I believe that one of the barriers to many women being comfortable with that fact and with those actions is that, for them, verbal communication is a form of control in what they perceive a relationship to be: a power struggle. And yet if that's true, and it is a power struggle, then husbands are generally easy to overpower! All a wife needs to do is tap into his physicality and she's won! Kelly, one of my listeners, figured this one out—to her pleasure, and to the benefit of her marriage:

> *"I believe that while women's needs are mostly emotional, men's are more physical. I make a point to take twenty minutes out of the day to connect intimately with my husband. Most women, I think, feel that with the demands children put on us twelve hours a day, this time with their husbands can be put on*

the back burner. This is a big mistake. By putting my marriage first, my two boys will ultimately benefit from a strong, happy, healthy foundation.

My husband is constantly telling me how lucky he is that we have regular 'alone time' (which meets part of my emotional needs), whether it leads to sex or we just give each other massages. Sometimes we just cuddle!

I think we are definitely not the norm in marriages today— and that is sad. Come on, women! What is twenty minutes a day? Give up the power struggle . . . you will be amazed at the results! Your emotional needs will be met and you just might get some extra help around the house!"

This issue of "power struggles" is at the core of many marital woes. The typical complaint from men: She nags and is never grateful or satisfied. The typical complaint from women: He's insensitive, doesn't meet my emotional needs, and won't do anything around the house. And it goes around and around and around as he becomes more disgruntled and she becomes more frustrated. Both husband and wife are unhappy.

Then they go to a therapist, but sadly, much of the psychotherapeutic profession is populated by folks with an agenda: Traditional values are out, men are the bad guys, and women are oppressed. Their cure is either to feminize the husband or suggest divorce. Ken, a listener, confirmed that position when he wrote:

"It has been my experience through nearly all the avenues we have tried (i.e., self-help books, tapes, private counseling, etc.) that today's society insists that it is COMPLETELY THE MALES' RESPONSIBILITY to learn how to understand and communicate on a level that the female can comprehend and digest. It seems that positive improvements to a relationship can ONLY occur if the husband is willing to alter his very nature, to

tune in to his 'feminine' side, and learn how to think, respond, and 'emotionally perceive' the same way his wife does.

If the male has any desires or perceptions that are different, it's only because of his selfish, obtuse, knuckle-draggin' nature, and it is up to him to cleanse himself of anything that might be termed 'masculine' if there is to be any peace in the house."

When I'm talking to wives on my radio program who feel desperate and depressed about what seems like a terminal situation, I ask them to do the seeming impossible: move forward with a new plan and a new attitude.

It's often hard for women to do that; like elephants, we have long memories . . . for hurt. Now, I do feel that there are some behaviors and actions that may defy forgiveness: cruelty, violence, addictions, and affairs. These problems are generally the exception, though, not the rule. I will ask the wife on the line if she chooses to be divorced. Generally, after considering her dreams, children, finances, and good memories, she'll say no. Then I'll suggest that she make a commitment to be different, in spite of old yucky memories or recent hurts.

After all, men can do some stupid things without even meaning to hurt. Jeff, a listener, revealed that in his letter:

"Women need to realize that we are just going to do stupid stuff. That doesn't make it malicious or a personal attack on them. When we do these stupid things, we don't need retaliation. We are usually embarrassed enough on our own. We need forgiveness.

We men will usually walk away from conflict with our wives without hostile thoughts, but unforgiveness on the woman's part will just hold them captive and build into more resentment. Forgiveness is the key to any successful relationship, in marriage or out, and sometimes you should give it if it is deserved or not."

I don't often use the word *forgiveness* in my radio conversations with callers; instead, I talk about *letting it go* so that one is able to grab on to something else, like hope. I remind women that although moving on doesn't mean that old, ugly memories and feelings won't pop up now and then, in both idle and stressful moments, still, they should not always act on them just because they feel them.

That is often a major revelation for them, to learn that not each and every thought and feeling needs to be revealed or acted upon. In fact, part of the maturity process is learning to choose what to deal with from within oneself, and what to take up with others. The alternative is to do what Gary, a listener, described:

> *"Women don't forgive well. They never forget—and stack disappointments up like cordwood. Women tend to blurt out, at what seems to be 'out of the blue' moments, being upset about what seem to be unrelated issues."*

This apparent lack of forgiveness is a weapon in that power struggle I mentioned earlier. That weapon is brandished for several important reasons:

- With the intent to hurt as payback for real or imagined hurts

- As a tool to demean in order to regain control

- As a means to turn the situation around, making the woman the victim when she is unwilling to take responsibility for what she's done wrong

The irony is that at the same time the woman wants to stay (happily) married, she traps herself into unhappiness by not "letting go" and "moving on."

Probably the first thing women need to forgive their husbands for is . . . for being men. Suzanne, a listener, wrote a long letter about the failure of her first marriage and what she learned that's making her second marriage, at thirty-seven years of age, work. Basically, she acknowledged that marriage is a lot of work and that the first thing she had to do is understand the difference between men and women. She explained that the problem, as she saw it, is that women want strong men who are good providers, but also expect them to be like a girlfriend they can always yak with: "We want them to be 'emotionally available.' In other words, WE WANT TO TURN THEM INTO WOMEN." She related a scene from a television movie she'd recently watched, where the husband, trying to console his wife, said, "I don't know what to do. You're not in any physical pain, which is the only pain a man understands." Suzanne wrote that she and her husband just about fell off the couch, they were laughing so hard.

Cary, another listener and husband, wrote:

> *"What I find interesting is that I am always accused of doing what always comes natural to a man. It would appear that my wife wants me to have the characteristics of a woman without losing my masculinity."*

He went on to describe some of the key points of contention between himself and his wife with respect to this expectation and communication. Frankly, they sound pretty universal:

- "I am told constantly that I do not ever listen. In most every case, I have listened—but I failed to read between the lines. Men are generally more black-and-white creatures. Men hate to try to read into everything. Women generally read into everything."

- "Women take offense at the smallest details and it frustrates them that men don't get hung up on every jot or tittle. They get the impression that we don't care."

- "Women generally like to talk and talk and talk and just vent about a problem. Men naturally and instinctively go into the solution mode and try to solve the problem and be done with it! We instinctively wish to protect our families and make sure their lives are secure. We wish only to help."

If women would simply look at their husbands as having characteristics instinctive to male nature, and not fight against those characteristics, they would find there would be less quarreling and fighting. Cary concluded by suggesting that women tend to fight against the natural characteristics of men more than men fight against those of women. I believe he's right.

The fact is that there will always be a power struggle between men and women in a "unisex"-mentality world. Only when women enjoy those strengths they have that men don't, and enjoy the strengths men have that they as women don't, will they be happier creatures and be able to play better in the sandbox called marriage.

One of the unfortunate sequelae of the feminist movement is a lack of respect for the uniqueness and specialness of femininity and masculinity. Many women are now fighting to regain their respect for their own femininity. That will certainly bode well for their ability to be able to accept and appreciate a man on masculine terms.

Sara May, one of my listeners, began that journey when she participated in a religious "Woman's Weekend." Through that experience she began to understand the basic differences between men and women, and how she was expecting things from her husband that he could not deliver. She also began to recognize that by demanding, criticizing, and being bitter, she was working against her vision of a happy, loving, long-term, growing-old-together relationship.

She decided to give those new concepts a try and reports that she feels very much in love in a deeper way than ever.

> *"I learned that the very thing that attracted me to him, his masculine, laid-back, quiet, kind demeanor, was what I was holding against him, instead of appreciating how those qualities enhanced our family—me being the more high-strung partner. I learned to create a brand-new list of everything about him that I loved and appreciated, conveyed my love and appreciation to him in small everyday acts, and made him feel that he was truly my hero.*
>
> *I felt the best of my femininity again . . . and so did he!*
>
> *I also learned to rely more on my female friends for the emotional connections I so craved and had wrongly expected my husband to provide for me, when it was not in his nature as a man to go to the depths that women are able to go on an emotional level."*

That means that if your husband doesn't *say* all the flowery things you think he should because you've watched too many chick flicks, you should look at what he *does*. When he scrapes the ice off your car windshield, that *is* love-speak. Men are made of action. Action is largely how men communicate.

Marge, a listener, described her husband as not overly affectionate or communicative, yet she's unbelievably satisfied with her marriage and deeply in love with what she feels is an incredibly loving man. How can that be? Simple. She's a smart woman—she understands that men demonstrate their emotions and passions in actions more than pretty phrases.

> *"He may not be able to tell me as often as I would like how head over heels in love with me he is or how incredibly beauti-*

ful I am. But he can call the tire place ahead of time, leave his workplace in the middle of the day, and meet me there with my car to get the new tires put on. I don't ask him to do it this way, he just does it—and he does it for me. I have come to appreciate that he has just shouted, 'I love you, baby!' to me in front of the whole tire place. I feel like a real queen. He has done these things for many years. I just had to open my eyes and appreciate them for what they are."

It is easy to challenge a husband when he says that his way of showing love is by going to work and earning money to provide for his family. Of course, he'd be working and battling traffic and corporate nonsense even if he were single. Yes, he would be doing the same thing, but not with the same commitment, intent, sacrifice, and depth of passion that he has when he's doing it for his woman and his children.

Men not only communicate with action and physicality, that's also how they receive messages of love. When a wife wraps her body around her husband's, in spite of being tired or frazzled from her day, he gets the message loud and clear that he is loved, wanted, appreciated, safe, and accepted. And as Cheryl, a listener, contributed so wisely: "When he feels loved and respected, the rest of his care and feeding is just a piece of cake."

When a wife wishes to communicate something important to her husband, the black-and-white approach is the most effective. That means forget the subtle hints. Mark, a listener, complained that "wives give hints and don't just say what they want. If I want something, I just say it. Wives have to beat around the bush and not just simply say, 'I want this. . . .'"

One listener wrote in that her husband always forgets anniversaries and birthdays. Instead of "getting mad and then getting even," she realized that this is not about his disregard for her—it's about his being a guy who doesn't much pay attention to specific details, but is always there for the bigger picture. She began talking months in advance of their anniversary:

> *"Subtle doesn't work for us. Saying, 'Wow! This will be twenty-five years on June 24. We should take a cruise.' Now, that works. We are going to Alaska!"*

Sadly, too many women get caught up in the absurdly romanticized notion that "if he loved me, he'd just know what I'm thinking, what I'd like, what he should say. . . ." Real life requires much more personal responsibility. One listener wrote in:

> *"For so long I expected my husband to read my mind. I thought, 'I can't believe he is asking me that! Doesn't he know by now what I like?' This would include everything from favorite colors to my favorite place for him to touch me during sex. I thought I could talk to him in some subtle, indirect way, and he would surely catch on. No, no, no. I have learned to say what I want and quit playing games that only leave us both frustrated."*

A husband's inability to read his wife's mind, judge her every mood, and be responsive to her every desire does not mean he doesn't love her or that he's an insensitive boob. It more likely means that he's just a normal guy.

And there are those times when these "just normal guys" want to communicate but don't . . . largely because they're afraid.

Men generally feel in a "damned if they do, damned if they don't" position. That means that if they don't say what's on their minds, they're condemned, and when they do say what's on their minds, they're condemned for "not saying the right thing."

Lloyd, a listener, sent me one hilarious letter about this problem:

"Wives continually remark, 'You never talk to me!' or 'You don't understand.'

But when husbands ask, 'What's wrong, honey?' we get, 'If you don't know, I'm not telling you!'

HUH?!

Women constantly and rightly point out that men aren't as sensitive to feelings as they are, but just as consistently completely ignore that wisdom.

If wives really want their husbands to understand them, they're going to have to acknowledge what they instinctively know and actually tell us what we need to know. Wives need to tell their husbands what they are thinking, feeling, and wondering about in simple, declarative sentences using one- or two-syllable words.

Examples:

Wife: Honey, I got my hair cut and styled today. Do you like it?

(Believe me, we men all know how to answer that one correctly.)

Not: Honey, do you notice anything different?

(Huh? Then she gets mad when we ask where the dog is.)

Or:

Wife: I want to go to the movies tonight.

Not: What do you want to do tonight, sweetie?

(Then stomp off into next week when we say, 'Just stay home and watch TV, honey.')"

Lloyd's bottom line is that he want wives to finally "get it" that men, whether husbands or bachelors, do not share their thoughts and feelings as readily as do women—frankly, they generally don't see any need to bother others with their feelings at all. They just deal with them. If something needs to be done, they do it. If something needs to be said, they say it. They largely just live with their thoughts and adjust.

But one big problem men have with opening up to their wives is that the consequences are often unpleasant, something I saw often in marital counseling sessions when I was in private practice. The wife would badger the poor, hapless fellow into revealing some feeling, then she'd pounce on it with a vengeance, accusing him of being completely wrong (with a feeling?), insensitive, stupid, mean, and so on.

That scene has risen to the level of justifiable stereotype. It got to the point where I would say in interviews that women only care about the feelings of their men when those feelings don't threaten them in any way (as in he "feels" she ignores him and spends all her time with her kids and being on the phone with her mother) or compliment them. Most wives don't really want to have to deal with their husbands' feelings, they just want to know that their husbands have positive feelings about them and that they feel for them, and so forth. Any other feelings of their husbands, which may not be pleasant for the wives to face or may be inconvenient to have to deal with, are generally squashed. Admit it. It's true. Many women are stuck in the "There shalt be no feelings before mine" mode. It's a self-centered position that has to be confronted and struggled with if there is to be any real compassion for the husband.

Glen's complaint was right on target:

"*Every authority in interpersonal relations says if you have a problem with your spouse, confront them with it. Talk to them and let them know how you feel. Whenever I try this, my wife responds with a very clear explanation of why I should not feel this way. She will share with me every reason why I am wrong to think the problem has anything to do with her!*

After thirty-five years of marriage, she cannot understand why I close myself up in my study and avoid any substantive discussion with her, why I don't share my feelings with her. I am not an idiot. I am a retired educator, with a thirty-year career behind me, who has, over time, been shrunken to a level of insignificance that is crippling.

I have loved my wife, raised three kids to adulthood with her, and have been completely faithful to her. Our lives would be so much better if she could listen and actually hear me rather than contemplate her 'defense' as I speak."

How painfully sad his letter was. All too often men will not speak because their wives will not let them say what they, the wives, don't want to hear. So the husbands are shut out. Then the husbands shut out their own feelings. Then they shut the wives out. I've received hundreds of letters from husbands expressing the same pain Glen did. It is remarkable that most of them still said they loved their wives and families, remained faithful, and didn't leave. Talk about the loyalty of an abused puppy!

And whether the husband is just being "a guy," or has actually backed off from communicating to his difficult wife, there is always the issue of the Patton-technique of getting a man to "open up." Roberto, "a guy" listener, wrote:

"One thing I find very frustrating is when my wife insists on digging out an answer or opinion when I'm not ready to talk— or I haven't figured out how to word the issue/opinion without her personalizing it. I believe that for most men, and I'm certainly in this category, it takes us time to process things verbally. Sometimes we need to start painting a room, play catch, or do something else physical to find the right words to convey, or decide to let it go and not 'die on that hill.' I just wish my wife would let me have time to think nonverbally."

Roberto's letter expresses an important position. I believe most wives simply want to be loving and helpful to their husbands, but when they don't take into account the "male" nature of their husbands, they often end up doing damage out of that good intention. Wives have a habit of questioning their husbands to death about their issues, feelings, etc. Men generally don't want an interrogation—open ears will do.

Since it's not in men's nature to "open up" about feelings, it's counterproductive to bombard them with questions and push, push, push. Let's get back to that "male physicality" point—mostly husbands just want to be heard, hugged, and supported. Which means don't overanalyze, or as Garry, a listener, wrote:

> *"Don't put everything a man says through a fem-filter and then expel what you believe is his real meaning. Men are never taken at their word; it all must be fem-filtered to find the true meaning of what it is that the man has said. Then he is blamed for the hurtful words that he never said in the first place!"*

Women should take whatever a man says at face value. Women tend to overanalyze men when men are just not that complicated. Wives need to give their husbands a break and respect that "guys" just have different ways without judging that difference as inadequate.

Charlie, another listener, points out this problem very clearly:

> *"The lack of respect for differing opinions seems to be a common frustration. What I find is an attitude from some women that if I think differently from them, it's because men are a-holes, or stupid, or just plain wrong. Name calling and insults are very difficult to ignore. I'm weary of sharing my opinions and feelings if I think there might be the slightest chance that they're not mainstream female points of view.*
>
> *And the sad thing is, when a man falls for this type of*

manipulation, and attempts to smooth out the rough male edges his wife despises, she's now even less attracted to the wimp she created!"

What follows are the common mistakes wives make in trying to communicate with their husbands. These were all submitted by male listeners:

- "Women are very good at dropping subtle hints when they want something. If I don't figure out what is wanted, then I am insensitive, uncaring, or oblivious. If they could make a simple request, like, 'Would you please do this or that for me?' it would give me a clear idea of what is expected. Also, women who espouse an acute sensitivity to feelings are often only sensitive to their own feelings and needs and not to their husbands'."

- "I don't know how to tell the difference between my wife wanting advice and just venting. For example, she will tell me that she has no time to fix dinner. I offer to take our sixteen-month-old daughter out for a walk. My wife will get upset that I don't understand. If she tells me a problem, I look for a solution. How can I know when I just need to listen . . . without dinner?"

- "I was married thirty-two years and then divorced. A man needs to know what a woman wants and needs before little things build up in reality or in her mind. A man is not a mind reader; don't nag, but you must be blunt sometimes. A wife needs to communicate the serious things in a special way so the husband will pay particular attention and not consider it just an ordinary, run-of-the-mill conversation. Do something different, like hold his hand and say, 'We need to discuss something very important to me.'"

• "A man wakes up in the morning with a clean slate and the thoughts in his head are something like this: 'Hmmm, what should I do today? I could work on my car, or the wife and I could go do something—I wonder what she wants to do? If she's busy, maybe I'll go find [friend's name] and see what he's doing. . . .' There's not a hint of malice there. So then the wife walks in and says something like, 'Well, what are you going to do today, work on the car all day in the shop? Well, fine, I'll just go find something else to do. You know, we never spend any time together anymore . . . blah, blah, blah.' What was the girl really trying to say? Probably, 'I'd like to spend some time together today with you, the man I love. I like to be with you and I miss you.' But what did the man get? 'I have already decided that you are uncaring and I don't have to take this!' What is the man's reaction? 'Heck, babe, I haven't even had my coffee yet. Why are you complaining about something that I haven't even done? I'm made to feel guilty of a crime I didn't commit, and whatever it is you want to do now, I feel manipulated into and will likely resent.' Women: Be direct!"

• "If there is something you wish to talk to us husbands about, begin with the subject. Don't work your way toward it; tell us up front you want to talk about, for example, discipline for the children, spending habits, or something about us you're dissatisfied with. Don't drop hints that are hard to follow or unintelligible. We need to be alerted to whether this is about small talk or something serious. For example: The wrong way is to say, 'How much did it cost you to play golf over the weekend? [Pause] Isn't that a lot for golf? [Pause . . . silence . . . lots of time . . .] Why won't you ever talk about money?' The right way is to say, 'We need to talk about money. I'm worried that we're spending too much.'"

• "Men are not mind readers. Many a time I have been in the situation where I have apparently done something wrong with no clue what it was or when it happened. I just know from the atmosphere in the house that something is not right. The silent treatment is a dead giveaway. When I ask my wife what is wrong, or what I did, the answer is always the same: 'Nothing.' Basically, I told my wife, 'I can't fix a problem if I don't know what it is.' Life is much better now."

It was heartening to read the many letters from wives who had turned the corner with many of the issues that the men brought up. Mary, a listener, had been married to her husband for ten years when (at forty-seven years of age) she started to take a long, hard look at how she treated him. She concluded that it was not his responsibility to read her mind. She used to think that because he was her husband, he should automatically and magically know how and what she felt and what her needs and desires were. She grew ashamed of how she'd let her expectations of him to read her mind allow so much hostility to creep into her mind and out her lips.

"It's amazing how I let myself get irritated if a laundry basket of his clean underwear and socks stayed at the foot of the stairs for days because I expected him to know that I thought he should put them away. Now I just tell him that the laundry in the basket is clean and ask him if he would please take it with him and put it away the next time he goes upstairs. And he does it with no problem!"

I believe that Mary hit upon something very important when she expressed awareness that her husband actually never intended to irritate her, and that a lot of what she was getting angry over was a result of how she interpreted his actions or inactions.

"You are right, Dr. Laura, the care and feeding of husbands is really a simple task. I had to stop complicating it with internal commentary."

Actually believing that a husband has a wife's welfare in mind, actually believing that he doesn't intend to hurt or disappoint, and being able to see the positive amidst the negative are the keys to the good feelings a wife can have about her husband. Kelly, a listener, wrote about her turning point with her husband over these issues. She remembered one argument (though she couldn't remember what it was about!), after which she stormed off to another room, and sat and stewed, thinking that if he loved her, he'd go out and buy her flowers, because he was the one who was wrong. She fumed and pouted every minute he didn't come in with flowers, thereby proving that he really didn't love her! Then she realized that this was getting them nowhere, that she was putting "winning" over her marriage.

She thought about what her husband would like and went out to the store to get him some chocolate milk and flowers. When she got back, they had a wonderful conversation about all the things they valued in each other, and realized how unimportant their disagreement had been.

"As simple as it sounds, treating a husband well hinges on the Golden Rule. Instead of stewing over what you're not getting and turning it into a tug-of-war (you demanding more, him pulling away defensively), try giving him some of what you'd like. Look at life from his perspective. It never hurts to come out and tell him how much you appreciate how hard he works to support the family, instead of just complaining that he's late for dinner again."

It's also important to not keep score with "gotcha" points of compliments. If you picked a good, decent man in the first place, you're going to get a lot of love reflected back to you if you concentrate on the giving rather than nag about receiving. You and your husband will be happier because your marriage will be stronger.

Alexis, a listener, wrote a very telling letter, which sums up this whole topic of communication. She talks about the way to properly care for and feed a husband, while at the same time getting what you want—assuming, of course, that what you want is reasonable. Alexis had an ongoing issue in her home, one that is ongoing in most homes: getting the husband to do something around the house, or to do *more* around the house, whether it be cleaning up or fixing up.

Alexis did what most wives do: argued, got angry, nagged, threatened, condemned, and punished. None of it worked. One day, when she was very fed up, she took a deep breath and asked her husband in a sincere, loving way, "You know, honey, when I ask you to do something around here, am I asking you to do too much? Are you doing as much as you could be doing or should I be doing this?" His response was, "No, I could be doing more." And all Alexis said was, "Okay."

> *"This could have turned into something big, but I just thought that we've argued about it so much and that just wasn't working. We women have to be smart. We need to make our husbands feel loved the way we want to feel loved. My husband's complaint before was that I kept track of everything he did wrong and what he didn't do. Men have feelings, too."*

And so Alexis's husband stopped trying to please her. She quickly changed her own tactics and began approaching him in a positive manner, as in, "That makes me so happy when you remember to take out the trash! Thank you very much!"

Now, it might make a wife wonder why she is thanking him for something he "should do," because, after all, it's his house, too, and women are not slaves . . . and here come all those negative thoughts and feelings to ruin the day. But the fact is, everyone deserves and needs appreciation and approval for what they do—whether it's their duty or not (or why do we give soldiers and other heroes medals?). As Alexis said:

"The more I acted positively and made a big deal about what he did do, the more he would do it. People will do more of what you praise them for. When I approach him like that, he's not defensive anymore."

By the way, her husband always starts his evening prayers now with, "Lord, thank you for my wife."

In conclusion, I give you Ron's list for wives who wish to communicate well and properly care for and feed their husbands and their marriages. He wrote that most women didn't realize how easy it is for them to get what they want from men. Here are the points he made:

• Men are impressed by honesty, not manipulation (nagging, coercing, yelling, crying, or emotional blackmail).

• If a wife's request gets too complicated, we tend to either forget or lose interest. So if wives can make sincere, short requests, we usually love making those requests happen.

• We love being able to expertly solve tough problems for those we love. If you treat us like the expert, we quickly become that, probably due to our need for ego strokes.

• Asking us anything in a loving manner will assure that you will quickly and easily put us into the mode of doing what you'd like. If there's enough real reward (appreciation, affection, approval, admiration), we will do almost anything for the source of the reward—almost as loyally as dogs.

• When you ask us to do something, be aware that distractions happen: Emergencies threaten and obstacles can become factors. If you remind us, again in that loving way, of your original petition we'll get back on track.

Gary, a listener, summarized all of the above with:

"The Proper Care and Feeding of Husbands? Be somebody he can respect. Then love him like you've never been hurt. And let him return the favor."

That's what needs the most communicating.

Chapter 6

WHAT'S SEX?

"I think women use their bodies as tools for controlling men. Once married, they go on to other tools. It seems to me we have this backwards. Girls ought to be more modest, and wives ought to be less so—around their husbands. Instead, single women show thighs and breasts, and wives dress like Eskimos. I saw a lot more skin in my dating life than I do as a married man—and I was a virgin when I married!"

BOB

"My wonderful wife has put it best: "Sex is to a husband what conversation is to a wife. When a wife deprives her husband of sex for days, even weeks on end, it is tantamount to his refusing to talk to her for days, even weeks." Think of it that way, wives, and realize what a deleterious impact enforced sexual abstinence has on a good man who is determined to remain faithful."

HERB

"We need more sex. Once a day is fine."

STEVE

If I were listing rules for the Proper Care and Feeding of Husbands, Rule One would be to . . . be a "girl." Sounds simple, doesn't it? Obviously, wives are female; women; girls. So what is there to actually "do" in order to be a girl? Lots.

After marriage, and definitely after having children, too many wives contract the "Frump syndrome," the symptoms of which include wearing flannel pajamas and socks, or sweat-pants with oversized T-shirts, to bed instead of some girly thing with lace; not shaving legs or grooming nails; not wash-ing, styling, or even combing hair; taking off (instead of fresh-ening up) makeup from the day just before your husband comes home; using the toilet with him in the room; not mak-ing an attempt to smell sweet (with a little perfume or body oil); and never putting on sexy outfits . . . in front of your hus-band.

When women have called in to my radio program to say that they are unhappy in their marriages, but nothing particu-lar is actually wrong, I ask them if they have contracted this ailment. Almost universally, the answer is yes. When I suggest the obvious cure, I am confronted with some angry, annoyed, resentful, defensive women! It's worrisome when women embrace the notion that once they are married, they are enti-tled to be loved, adored, protected, gifted, romanced, obeyed, and provided for without question, without reciprocation, and definitely without any effort on their part to create the emo-tional and psychological environment that would more likely get them all those desires.

Sam, a female listener, wrote:

"Women expect to be wooed yet be allowed to look haggish and frumpy. It's hard to romance a hag and come off as being sincere. I will admit that I have fallen into the trap of letting myself go, but I have been clawing my way out of that hole. I now put the extra effort into showering and doing my hair and makeup before my darling comes home from work, and well, it has certainly paid off!"

As if in rebuttal, the wives will give themselves amnesty because, "He . . . (something to criticize him for)." "Well," I'll say, "that may be so. But you're the one calling me, unhappy. And you're the one who can decide to make this situation better." I remind them that "men are simpler," and that they, the wives, really have the power to change what is happening in the relationship because, as I've said earlier, men forgive easier and are more easily corrected in their behaviors with positive feedback than women are.

What attracts men to women is their femininity, and femininity isn't only about appearance, it's also about behaviors. Looking womanly and behaving sweetly and flirtatiously are gifts wives give to their husbands. This gift communicates that the husband is seen as a man, not just a fix-it guy, the breadwinner, or the sperm donor. And if it's romancing a wife is hungering for, presenting oneself as an appealing "woman" will get more romancing than presenting oneself as only a child-care worker, or house cleaner, or the other wage earner.

Kelly, a listener, wrote that she remembered how much effort she put into her femininity when she was dating her now-husband. She would look forward to cooking him romantic meals, and buying sexy outfits to flounce around in. She loved the way he "wanted" her and she loved the feeling of wanting him.

After marriage, there were bills to pay, two careers, a home to keep up, and children to raise. After the second child she gave up her career to take care of the home and children. She would spend the day cleaning, doing laundry, grocery shopping, playing with the kids, and balancing the checkbook. When her husband came home, immediately there were things she wanted him to do . . . now! And, of course, none of those things had anything to do with romance, intimacy, or any other lovish activities.

She discovered that she was becoming more naggy, hostile,

and bitter, with a growing feeling that she was being cheated out of life. When her husband came home, she stopped going to the door with a hug and a kiss, stopped showing affection, stopped having sex, and even stopped the good-night kiss.

Basically, she was blaming her husband for her unhappiness, insisting that it was up to him to go out of his way to please her and pamper her to make up for how difficult her life was. Never mind how difficult his day was—which was only amplified by his wife's angry discontent.

It was only when a female relative came to ask Kelly for advice about marriage that she realized she was not practicing what she was preaching. She acknowledged to herself that she was using her husband as a scapegoat for her own emotional struggles, and was so busy blaming him for what she felt he was not giving her that she wasn't noting what she wasn't giving him.

> *"I am on the road to fixing that. For starters, I began by realizing how lucky I am that I have the ability to stay at home and raise my boys. I wouldn't have that luxury if it weren't for my husband's hard work. I still have that excitement to do things to make him happy because it also makes me happy. I give, he gives. I give more, he gives more. I realized that it isn't all about what I'm not getting, it's about what I'm giving that makes the difference."*

There are two important issues in Kelly's letter: appreciation for what one has and the realization that giving begets getting. And it needs to be emphasized that the most important thing a wife has to give to her husband is herself; therefore that "self" needs to be taken care of and then shared. That a wife cleans the house or drives the kids all over town or argues a big court case is all wonderful, but it's not giving of herself to her husband. While fulfilling the obligations and responsibilities of taking care of the house and family is an essential part of giving in a marriage, other folks could be hired to do it. The real essence of giving is more intimate, sensitive and vulnerable, and up close and personal. Since fidelity is an essential part of trust and commitment, no one can or should be hired to take care of any of the tender, loving, sensual, sexual aspects of marriage!

Romancing a spouse is supposed to be a two-way street, but I'm wracking my brain trying to think of one movie, book, play, or conversation on the radio, when I've heard a man describe his wife as romantic. I can't think of one time. Is it that men don't need romancing? No, don't believe that. Is it that men define romancing differently? Probably. Is it that men don't get much romancing? Definitely.

But let's first go back to the differences in defining romancing in the minds of men when it pertains to their actions or their wives'. When men think of being romantic, they think of what women like: sweet words, flowers, perfume, dinners out, and gifts. When men think of women being romantic toward them, they think less of what she can go out and buy or specifically do; they think more of how she presents herself to him as a woman and how she reinforces his ego by treating him as desirable and competent. It's how she makes him feel like a real man and her hero.

In order for a wife to do that, she's got to tune out of herself and tune in to him. For many wives it means tossing out their bags of petty, bitter feelings, resentments, disappointments, and overreactions to basic annoyances. While that is often a daunting task, the rewards are worth it in the long run.

It might seem that I'm suggesting that men are totally superficial, requiring that their wives look like *Playboy* centerfolds, and while that's a popular stereotype, my research in preparation for this book demonstrates otherwise. It's not "absolute perfection" that men desire from their wives (although a "10" walking by will get any man's attention); it's the effort the wives put in to pleasing their men that seems to make the most impact. That's not a superficial concept. It means that men appreciate that their wives care about their "male nature," which responds dramatically to visual stimulation.

One husband wrote:

> *"Almost every man I've ever spoken to is not infatuated with big breasts (even though women are). They don't find attractive the terribly skinny models featured in women's magazines. They like normal, naturally shaped women, much like Jennifer Lopez or Marilyn Monroe. They like women who are naturally attractive, what many women would consider plain-looking. Men generally don't like a lot of makeup. What many men are concerned about is if their wives let themselves go, gaining huge amounts of weight.*
>
> *Men actually find their wives' bodies attractive, though, even when they carry a little extra weight. Husbands have an intrinsic need to enjoy their wives' bodies 'visually' for their emotional well-being. And both men and women have a responsibility to keep their appearance up, within reason."*

Frankly, men like to look at their wives' bodies naked, watch the simple act of them undressing, see them in something sexy. Men need this visual excitement, and they should get it from their wives, not from adult bookstores or the Internet. The men who wrote to me commenting on this issue surprisingly were in agreement that there was no absolute rating system in their minds about perfect female bodies when it came to their wives. Most of the men were describing their desire for their wives to dress (and undress) and behave somewhat coquettishly. Their sense of well-being was very tied into their wives indulging them with visual input and seductive behavior.

Ralph, a listener, expressed his frustration with his wife's just not caring about this part of his being:

> *"The number one thing my wife doesn't do is take care of her-self. After the courting and the 'I do's,' attention turns to other things. On your radio show, when you get a caller who is now less interested in their relationship, you advise them to go back to what attracted their mate in the first place. For guys that is generally to be romantic, bring flowers, take her to an exciting place, etc. For women, it is to fix themselves up, put on some-thing nice, and be sweet.*
>
> *Guys have a natural and deep desire to be with a woman who cares enough about herself to look good for her mate."*

In reading all the letters from men, I was struck by their depth of sensitivity about the issue of women's appearance. It wasn't an impersonal, animal reaction (as it is with women the men don't personally know), it was a deeply personal one. The wife's comfort with and appreciation of her own body and femininity, and her willingness to share that with her husband, actually fed his sense of well-being, his feeling of being loved as a husband and valued as a "man."

Shahina, a listener, wrote about her sad story of divorce after ten years of marriage. Her husband left her, complaining that they had so little time together (because she was over-involved with her "mommy and daddy") and he no longer found her attractive. It seems she had gained a tremendous amount of weight by eating too much and exercising too lit-tle. I can bet that the reaction of most women upon reading that is to get their hackles up and proclaim her husband as shallow. Frankly, that hostile reaction itself demonstrates a shal-low self-centeredness. The impact on our bodies of natural aging, illness, pregnancies, and so forth is a simple fact of life. The inability to accept these realities betrays immaturity or

worse. At the same time, though, the unwillingness to accept
responsibility for the upkeep of one's physical or emotional
well-being should be met with consternation by a spouse
because it is an assault on the marital covenant. And the disregard of the unique feelings and needs of one's spouse is a selfish insult.

Shahina's letter went on to say:

*"I would try to tell him that I would go on a diet and exercise
to lose weight and become more attractive. I thought I would do
these things for him so that he would find me attractive. I knew
deep down that I did not want to do those things because I
wanted him to love me and accept me just the way I was."*

This is not an unusual sentiment for me to hear from
women, who express hostility that their husbands would like
them to clean up, dress up, and tone up. They act like their
husbands are selfish, sex-crazed, superficial, insensitive barbar-
ians, which isn't the case. The "If they loved me, they wouldn't
make a fuss about such things" point of view is simply irresponsible and destructive. As I said in my chapter on communication, verbal exchange is but one means of communication.
A lot is also said by one spouse to another by the willingness
to fulfill each other's needs. Men have the emotional need to
see their wives as desiring them, and the way the wives take
care of and present themselves expresses that love.

The natural extension of these positive attitudes and behaviors is sexual intimacy. Phil, a listener, introduces us to this
issue beautifully:

*"God made men the way they are; men have hormones and
urges. I believe that too many women think that men are over-
sexed, but in this area men are not self-made. For men, it does
not take a super sex partner to keep a man happy. Making love
with the wife, even at low frequency, keeps a man healthy and*

home. But when sex is withheld, the need for and lack of it becomes a constant state of mind for men. It forces men to turn their thoughts outward.

I believe that most men would not settle for a fast-food burger when they have prime rib at home, but when they are hungry, they will find a way to get fed. I believe that most men do not want to leave their wives—they are driven out by a lack of physical love, compassion, and understanding in the area of sexuality."

Male sexuality is yet another subject that seems to elicit hostility in many women. Much of that hostility is the product of defensiveness resulting from the realization that they, the women, indeed are not putting their husbands' needs anywhere prominent on their to-do lists. Kim, a listener, got that straightened out fast when her husband came to her and asked her if a divorce would make her happy. She was shocked! She could not understand what he meant because she felt extremely happy with her life, her marriage, and her children. She immediately suspected that he had a girlfriend, but that wasn't the case. The truth was, he thought *she* must be getting her sexual satisfaction somewhere else because she rejected him sexually just about all the time.

He went on to tell her that he loved her and wanted her to be truly happy and that he was sorry if he failed in doing this. According to Kim:

"The truth was I had an excuse every time he wanted to be intimate. I'd say, 'I'm tired,' or 'The only time you show affection is in the bedroom,' or 'I just don't feel like it.'"

Her husband then confessed to her that he had looked at pornographic pictures on the Internet. Kim's first reaction was disgust, then deep hurt . . . then humility as he explained to her that as empty and guilty as he felt while doing that, still it was easier than coming to bed only to be rejected again. He told her that she's the only one he wants but she won't let him have her. He said that he was frustrated by the intensity of his desire for her, and wished he could be neutered like a dog to diminish his suffering.

He remarked that being rejected is always bad, but being rejected when one is at his most vulnerable—naked—is devastating. Kim wrote:

> *"I was saddened and humbled by my lack of selflessness. Yes, every day I give to my kids, my home, my friends, and even to myself in many different ways, but I have failed to give in the right ways to the most important person in my life: the person who makes my life complete, happy, and possible—my best friend—my husband.*
>
> *My truth: Before I was married I used sex to get what I wanted. Now I have what I've always wanted (more than I deserve) and see sex as useless. I have taken him for granted and pushed aside his emotional and physiological needs."*

"I've pushed aside his emotional and physiological needs." That is a powerful admission. Since that time, Kim has changed her priorities. She now pays attention to her husband as a man. She writes that he is incredibly good looking, fit, and a great dad. Since she's begun to look at him with a "new eye," she's grown more in feelings of love and begun to see the sexiness that she missed for so long. She reports that the children's bedtime has changed from nine to eight, all electronic devices are turned off, and "the house is rocking!"

Still, it is astonishing the extent to which female society denigrates a man's sex drive, reducing him to merely a rutting animal with no deeper context. After reading all the mail from men about the Proper Care and Feeding of Husbands, though, there's no way to hold that position.

Most men actually pointed out in their letters that their desire for sex wasn't just about a "release" (although that is a great need for both men and women). As Chris, a listener, wrote:

"I don't understand why women don't understand that sex is a man's number one need from his wife. It's not just the act and sensation of pleasure, but it's the acceptance by a woman of her man. There's a communion that happens during intercourse that will bond a man to his woman, and he in turn will then begin to give of himself emotionally to her.

When that need isn't met, the man begins to look at his wife as just a roommate who doesn't pay her share of the rent but continues to harp on him about leaving the toilet seat up."

Ron, another listener, describes himself as a romantic, sensitive, and helpful husband who believes that women need to be more open to discussing sex rather than immediately dismissing all men as just "sex hounds."

"I am tired of women putting all men down for wanting and needing affection. Aren't people in love supposed to want to kiss, hug, and make love? That just makes sense to me."

Ron pointed out that sex and affection are healthy ways for couples to connect and should be given freely and eagerly in a good relationship. He believes that if women thought sex and affection were as important as any other part of a marriage, there would be fewer breakups because there would be more mutual satisfaction and bonding.

Jessica wrote with a critical female perspective on this issue:

"You're willing to scoop poop off of chubby baby thighs, clean vomit out of cars/car seats, wipe colorful snot off of drooling

children's noses . . . I think you can be willing to have sex with your husband!"

A stay-at-home mother, Jessica belongs to a number of groups, and the talk about sex is always anti-male. She wrote that the majority of the women are just tired and see their husbands as selfish for "wanting some." She reminds them that they are communicating negative messages to their husbands when they're willing to get up several times during the night for their child but act like spending a few minutes nurturing their husbands is such an unnecessary chore.

> *"I think that there is a myth out there that men need to ejaculate. I asked my husband, 'If I just lay there and let you get your physical needs met, is that satisfactory? Is that what you need?' He was disgusted! He wants to interact with me. He wants me to participate with him. This is not just a matter of a physical outlet for him.*
>
> *I also asked him, 'After we have sex, do you feel physically relieved, or closer to me, or happy about our family, or just totally blank or relaxed/stress free?' His reply was that he feels good about his family and our relationship."*

I wonder how many women have the guts to ask their husbands that question . . . and respect the answer?

In addition to the obvious physical pleasure involved, men desire sex in order to feel emotionally closer to their wives. So perhaps more wives should say, "All my husband wants is to feel close to me," instead of "All my husband wants is sex from me." That would make it much harder to dismiss the husband and his unique male sexuality. Sex is the way men communicate their emotions to and about their wives.

When wives are hostile or rejecting about sexual intimacy and physical affection, men begin to believe that their wives no longer have interest in them in any personal, profound way. How lonely, how neutered will a man feel before disconnecting from his wife altogether? Ron, a listener, says:

"I believe that most wives who feel secure in their marriages believe that because their husband loves them, they no longer need to address the sexual part of the marriage like they did in the beginning. What most men want is a wife who still desires her husband, and the fulfillment of that is the closeness in the sexual experience. From a man's point of view, if this does not happen, his communication, moods, and masculine well-being suffer."

Another listener, Don, wrote that as a man, he seeks out intimacy with his wife as a means of expressing his love, as well as his desire to put aside any small differences that have cropped up. To be turned down is extremely hurtful, and is very harmful to the relationship because as wives remove the opportunity to experience that depth of closeness, both physical and emotional, men find themselves losing all positive and caring feelings toward their wives. Yet wives expect husbands to ignore their own neglected needs and hurt feelings and do for them whatever they want . . . or else.

Mike's letter was one of the most touching I received. He began by saying:

"Dr. Laura, you have been openly supporting husbands. And that is contrary to the popular 'man-bashing' that I usually have to endure. Because of this I will share my thoughts on this topic."

Mike went on to describe himself as forty-four years old, with three children, all adults. He is in his second marriage, with a woman who already had two adult children. He talks about the care and feeding that he needs in order to "feel like a man." Mike sees his role as providing for and protecting his family, and is willing to work as hard as it takes to do both. He says that the appreciation he needs can come from a kiss at the door, or his wife reaching for his hand or drawing him into a hug.

> *"When I feel that my wife feels safe in my arms, then I know that I am doing my job. To be desired is an extension of this closeness."*

Unfortunately, he reports that affection and physical intimacy are gone from the relationship—and he doesn't know why. He reaches out to her, but only coldness and rejection are returned.

> *"When I am feeling the most rejected, I ask myself, 'Why am I here?' and 'Who cares for me?' To me, I am still doing my job of protecting and providing, but I get nothing in return.*
>
> *When months pass without sex or affection, the message that I get is that I am undesirable and have no value. If I were appreciated, I would be 'loved.' Caring and nurturing is what I need to feel healthy and happy."*

I get so many letters like Mike's, and it tears up my heart to read about the depth of hurt men feel from their wives' sexually rejecting them. This isn't physical frustration, it's real emotional hurt.

Interestingly, one male listener wrote that when wives constantly belittle and neglect their husbands' sexuality, the men become emotionally suppressed and then their wives don't get what they need from them. He further indicted that he believes these women are displaying the "moral equivalent of infidelity." This latter statement deserves some attention. When we normally think of infidelity, we think of a spouse having an emotional and/or sexual relationship outside of the marriage, whether with a "real honey" or a "synthetic honey" on the Internet. That is an obvious breach of marital vows as well as a violation of one of the Ten Commandments. However, don't the marital vows include and imply words like *love, honor, protect, care for,* and so forth? So when one breaches those vows by neglect, is that not also a form of infidelity? Perhaps we should start looking at the act of intentionally depriving a spouse of his legitimate needs as infidelity, too, because it stems from being unfaithful to the intent of the vows.

Sex is a serious point of contention for many women. I can remember one female caller in particular who complained that her husband wasn't understanding about how tired, burdened, and overwhelmed she was. He still wanted sex. I asked her what was wrong with that since most people expect monogamy in marriages, not celibacy. That seemed to startle her . . . but only for a moment.

She hit me back with the challenge, "Should I be expected to have sex when I don't want to just because he wants to?" I took a deep breath and answered, "Most of the time, yes." She was horrified and likened my response to a call for some form of slavery. I reminded her that she expected him to go to work and earn money to support the family even on days he didn't feel like it. I added that she expected him to visit her relatives whether he liked them or not, or was even treated very well by them. I threw in that she expected him to submit to her decisions regarding their social calendar in spite of his personal preferences. "It's called," I reminded her, "loving obligation." This time she was quiet a little longer.

I then went on to ask her about the times she "didn't feel like it" but did it anyway:

DR. LAURA: Didn't you get turned on at some point in the lovemaking?

CALLER: (giggling) Yes.

DR. LAURA: Well then, sometimes the pump just needs a little priming. . . . And didn't you feel great about him and life in general after a good orgasm?

CALLER: (giggling again) Yes.

DR. LAURA: Then why the hell would you want to keep that from your own life? Never mind for a moment that you've been suffocating your husband. Think about what you've been missing! Don't cut off your nose to spite any part of your body!

So many women seem to get so compulsive about everything else in their lives besides intimacy with and compassion toward their husbands. Of course, regular sex is not in and of itself the panacea for troubled marriages or troubled spouses. But if women would show more compassion for a man's physical needs, they would find themselves happier and better able to survive and confront all the annoying challenges of life.

When women call complaining that they are turned off to their husbands because the men seem to have a never-ending need for sex and only do affectionate things when they want sex, I remind them of something one of my listeners, Clint, wrote in:

> *"She says that I don't want to cuddle her without having sex, because I get aroused when we touch. I say that if someone is starving and you put a plate of food in front of them, you can't expect them to just nibble on it. Give them a full stomach, then they will snack."*

Based upon that concept, I have told wives that the way to cut down on their husbands' seemingly voracious appetite for sex is to take control by initiating sex play themselves—and at reasonably frequent intervals. When these women call me back, they all report the same results: (1) They're having more fun in their lives, (2) they feel closer to their husbands than ever before, and (3) their husbands don't seem to be nagging about sex at all.

Magic.

Douglas added his opinion:

"If you are not really interested in having sex at a certain time but your husband is, say something to the effect of, 'Come on, big guy. Show me what you got. Let's do it just for you.' Then tell him to skip the foreplay on you and just do his thing. Be extra enthusiastic and active. He will come sooner and think you are terrific. You might even find that you yourself are more interested in having an orgasm that you thought!"

But remember, do it with enthusiasm. As Scott wrote:

"What's worse than rejection is a begrudged spreading of the legs so we can get it over with and go to sleep. How is a man supposed to feel like he is pleasuring his wife with an attitude like that? The most pleasure a man can get from sex is to know he is pleasing his wife."

It ought to seem obvious that when you love someone, you aim to please them and make them feel loved and contribute to their happiness. One listener, Michele, was quite blunt about this by saying that although she might not always be "in the mood," she is always ready when he wants it.

"It may sound stupid, ladies, but I want to make sure he gets what he wants. He's too wonderful and I love him too much to disappoint him. That's how I nurture and respect my husband: communication, understanding, support, great chocolate chip cookies, and GREAT SEX!"

Now, honestly, does Michele sound oppressed and miserable? I'm convinced that most of the oppression women experience is of their own making—through their misguided choices and attitudes.

Lounelle, another listener, concurs with Michele's positive attitude:

> *"I have felt like sex is the last thing on my mind for different reasons, but it never fails that if I give in and enjoy the attention my husband shows me that my attitude changes, and not just for the moment."*

Barbara wrote to me after hearing a particular female caller on my radio program who didn't want to give her husband sex because she said she wasn't getting the little displays of affection from him she needed to make her feel good. Barbara was stunned that she recognized herself in that call! She had begun to resent the sex her husband always seemed to want, and because of her actions, her husband didn't feel very affectionate with her and didn't do those little things she wanted, which only served to increase her resentment . . . and so it went around and around! Barbara described herself as pretty cold and aloof, acting most of the time like sex was a chore and hoping he would just get it over with. But then she changed. . . .

> *"Man, oh man, did the affections get showered all over me. I began realizing how incredible my husband was, and my prayer and devotion life in the morning began to center around being a better wife and then mother. I began to look forward to seducing my husband, and he was so amazed that he felt that he had a new wife! He began again to show me all the affection that I missed from the beginning of our marriage because I once again showed him how much I loved him.*
>
> *Your caller cannot expect her husband to shower her with affection when she is so resentful of the intimate part of their life that means so much to him."*

My on-air conversation with Anna, twenty-five years old, married for five years and with two children, one five and the other nine months, provided me with one of the most startling exchanges concerning marital sex.

After she became a mother, Anna was worn out and didn't much feel like having sex. That is not unusual for new mothers, considering the hormonal changes and the challenges of little sleep and the relentless needs of a new baby. Nonetheless, affection between parents at this time is important on so many levels: Their bond needs to be confirmed, they need each other's support and tenderness to help with the transition from "us" to "family," and they could both benefit from the fun and release that sex offers.

In Anna's case, she rejected her husband so often that she got sick of doing it. Her solution? She told him that she would pay for him to seek out a prostitute. Now, four years later, he told her that while he followed her instructions, he wasn't able to go through with anything once he thought of their daughter. Neat guy.

DR. LAURA: What is your question for me?

ANNA: I just don't know if I should end the relationship.

DR. LAURA: You want to dump a man with whom you have two small children because you refused to have sex with him and told him to have sex with a prostitute? He tries to do what you told him to do, but he didn't really go through with much of it, and he tells you four years later, and you want to dump him? Frankly, of the two of you, he looks better.

ANNA: He should have understood me.

DR. LAURA: Anna, one of the big mistakes women make is to think that because he marries you, he's obligated to stay there, obediently and docilely, no matter how you treat him. Of course being a new mother is difficult. But isn't being a new father difficult in its own

way? When you tell a man that you disdain him intimately enough that you can't be bothered to hug,
kiss, or make love, for any reasons, in an ongoing way,
and then tell him to go pay someone else for sex and
leave you alone—but you still expect him to come
home and love, cherish, support, and understand
you—then you've got wires loose.

This call had a positive ending. I reminded her that she hurt
him first and that, because he loved her, he was not holding
that above her head. She agreed with that. I also reminded her
that he wanted to have a long, wonderful life with her and that
she needed to return that favor by never throwing this incident in his face again.

ANNA: You're right.
DR. LAURA: So when he comes through the door, I
expect some slurpy kisses, a good, hot dinner for him,
and, uh, you know, put the kids to bed early.
ANNA: Thank you so much, Dr. Laura.

Women, as Anna expressed, expect their men to be understanding about them not being in the mood for sex. But women
need to reciprocate that understanding and not be critical when
their husbands desire *them*. Likewise, they need to get it into
their heads that their husbands are not just "wantin' some," they
are desiring closeness with and acceptance by them!

"Accepting" a husband's sexual/affectionate advance is not
the only way a wife can lovingly demonstrate her openness
and caring. How 'bout actually being the aggressor! Jeffrey, a
listener, wrote for all husbands:

*"PLEASE be the sexual aggressor almost 50 percent of the
time. If you chase him around the house/bedroom/bed enough,*

he will be too tired, and pleased, to even give another woman a passing thought . . . well, a good man won't.

Do you know what it means to a man to hear his woman say aloud the words 'Would you please make love to me?' or 'Would you please————' (you fill in the blank with some sexual invitation). Don't spend a lot of time in front of the mirror wishing you were something you are not. Your husband is likely not a movie star either, and he loves you anyway.

Your 'sexual personality' determines a lot in how your husband sees you. The most beautiful woman in the world who says 'no' all the time to any and all sexual suggestions or overtures becomes ugly in his eyes in a big hurry. A supposedly 'plain'-looking woman who is a more-than-willing love partner with a good imagination in the bedroom, living room, shower, backseat, secluded woods, etc. (you get the idea), becomes one of the most beautiful women in the world.

Please, PLEASE, if we aren't doing something right sexually—PLEASE communicate. Go ahead, whisper naughty and loving things in our ears, we'll take your lead. And say 'I love you.' What? You thought only women love to hear that?"

A lot of women have called my radio program telling of their reluctance to "ask for some" or to "ask for it to be done a bit differently." It's understandable—nobody wants to look foolish or risk rejection. But remember, that's the same emotional issue that your husband has! *He* has to communicate one way or another and risk *your* response.

And don't worry about looking "slutty" to your man. Not one of the hundreds and hundreds of faxes and e-mails from men included the notion that if a man's wife "came on" to him, he'd be dismayed or horrified. The universal response was one of great longing and potential glee.

In addition to all the good that can come from the wife being more available, agreeable, open, experimental, and seductive (i.e., sharing more responsibility for the marital love life), there is also that building up of the male ego, which contributes a lot to a husband's sexual satisfaction. It's that "hero" thing again. As one woman wrote:

> *"When Viagra hit the market and everyone was talking about it, a friend asked my husband if he was using it. I quickly responded, 'Are you kidding? They come to our house to get his blood to make the stuff!' He beamed with delight and saw that I considered him as he was twenty years ago and began to act the part!"*

She ended her letter with something very touching and interesting. She talked about a Bible verse:

> *" 'Faith comes by hearing. . . . ' If we say hateful things about each other, we begin to believe it and it just keeps escalating until our 'faith' in our marriage is over."*

Her husband wakes her up each morning calling her his Proverbs 31 Woman. And every day, she reports, she tries to live up to it. That means she builds him up so he can be on the same kind of pedestal he's put her on. How beautiful a sentiment is that?

Helen, another listener, has two rules when it comes to sex in her marriage. First, she never turns her husband down. She describes him as very passionate and someone who likes to make love several times a week.

> *"Unless I have just had major surgery, or am very, very angry with him, I don't turn him down. I am past forty and, honestly, I have found my own drive diminishing. Dr. Laura has said on her show that even if you are not in the mood, once you start it, it's fun. She's right! I don't want him hesitant to approach me,*

nor do I want him looking elsewhere. He knows his wife, lying right next to him in his bed, is always warm and eager."

Helen's second rule about married sex has to do with "experimentation." Evidently, her husband is quite creative. When he tries something new, she doesn't let her first reaction be one of rage or disgust without considering the possibility of it being something she might like, and maybe giving it a go. She says she draws the line at pain and other people, but believes that the creative side of their lovemaking is part of their exploring possibilities together.

But let's get back to that problem of diminishing desire. It is not an issue of normal aging, and any woman who leaves it at that is fibbing. Ask her about her lustful fantasies about some suave, buffed-up movie star or neighbor. It is true that when life gets routine and mundane, the excitement is often replaced by a kind of sad lethargy. Some of that is good, as it makes life more comfortable. But some of it isn't good, because it makes life predictably boring. That's when you've got to get into gear and do something.

Lisa, a listener, was precisely in that "bored, tired, uninterested" place. When she got into bed at the end of the day, she only wanted sleep, but her husband "bugged" her about sex. Then one rainy afternoon, she called her husband at work and said that it was the perfect day for him to come home early and crawl into bed with her. Even though he couldn't, because he had an important meeting scheduled that he couldn't get out of, later he told her that he couldn't stop thinking about her all day and couldn't wait to get home to her. How many wives hear that after fourteen years of marriage?

It's got to be ego-boosting to have a husband still "want" his wife, to find her desirable even with her varicose veins, stretch marks, and C-section scars. Women often talk about being depressed about their lives, but if they would only jump-start their sexual interaction with their husbands, and be lavished with all that emotional and physical feedback, I think that would beat any Valium cocktail they might consider taking.

Sex, like any other part of the marital relationship, needs respect and nurturing. So no TV in the bedroom—keep it a beautiful sanctuary. The bedroom is the foundation of the marriage and family. Don't underestimate its importance and its power to generate the energy by which every member of the family flourishes.

Chapter 7

A MAN SHOULD BE RESPECTED IN HIS OWN HOME

"My father's advice when I married was, 'You are marrying a man. Always treat him like one and he will always act like one.'"
TAMMY

"It is easy for a woman to love; that is the way that God made her. It is more difficult for her to show respect."
WENDI

"I think men need respect—and the more respect they're shown, the more love they give in return."
JANETTA

The day before I began this chapter, I received a call on my radio program from a husband and wife together. The husband began the conversation by telling me of the latest in a series of typical incidents involving his mother-in-law. Frankly, the wife's behavior and point of view stunned me into silence!

It seems the husband, wife, and several children had gone to

Grandma's house for dinner. Afterward they all left in separate cars to come back to the callers' home. For some reason, the car with Grandma and some of the children stopped in a parking lot of a large department store. The twelve-year-old boy, suffering from a bad cold, needed to clear his throat of some mucus, which he spit out on the parking lot ground. Evidently, Grandma went ballistic, yelling at him that he was "no better than someone from the ghetto."

When everyone arrived at the callers' home, one of the daughters turned to Grandma and told her that it wasn't nice of her to hurt her brother's feelings. The twelve-year-old was crying.

Dad got into gear and started questioning Grandma about her behavior, and she immediately got defensive and hostile, eventually "flipping the bird" at Dad. At this point, according to the father, he told his mother-in-law in no uncertain terms that she was not going to disrespect him in his own home!

I asked the wife if she concurred with her husband's rendition of events. While she agreed that he'd described the events accurately in a general way, it was stunningly clear that her loyalties lay with her mother. For example, she criticized her son for coughing up on the parking lot ground, where "other people have to walk." She also said that her husband had raised his voice excessively. Clearly, she was most motivated to justify her mother's (mis)behaviors.

I was surprised, quite frankly, to hear a mother not jump to the defense of her child; sadly, I am more used to wives not jumping to the defense of their husbands, especially when their "mommies" are involved. When I addressed her condemnation of her son ("He was choking on sputum—a glass of water or a paper towel could have been used to clean up without embarrassing the boy"), her reaction was to discount this suggestion and to reiterate her mother's position that the boy was "bad."

The real stunner was when she turned on her husband. In the most horrible, disdainful, sarcastic manner, she imitated him saying, "A man should not be disrespected in his own home." She particularly emphasized "man" and "own home" with her snotty disregard for him.

I quietly said, "You *don't* think a man should be respected in his own home?" She flippantly came back with, "I think everyone should be respected everywhere." I repeated, "You *don't* think *a man* should be respected in his own home?" She wouldn't answer that.

I tried to reach her, but frighteningly, she clearly saw nothing wrong with her manner or attitude. After the call, I expressed out loud that I felt deeply sorry for this man and his children.

Another female caller the day before did "get it." She and her husband already had a cat, when she decided to get a second one. He strongly protested about getting another animal in the house. She called me to find a way to convince him to agree to what she wanted.

DR. LAURA: What? He doesn't have the right to his position?

CALLER: Yes, of course he does. It's just that I don't see any good reason to not have another cat.

DR. LAURA: A good reason is that he doesn't want to live with multiple animals. Why isn't that a good enough reason?

CALLER: Can't I keep pushing him to specify his reasons? Doesn't he have to justify his position? I just want to know why he feels that way.

DR. LAURA: No, you don't. You are not really interested in *understanding* his position. You just want him to enumerate his arguments so you can shoot them down so that you can have the cat. You don't want to "understand," you ultimately want to "manipulate." In general, men are more easily beaten down by the relentless arguments of their wives than the reverse.

CALLER: Yeah, I guess that's so. But I really want this other cat!

DR. LAURA: Obviously, you want that cat more than you want to show your husband respect and love.

CALLER: No, that's not so.

DR. LAURA: Yes, it is—and you know it. You aren't simply grateful and satisfied with one animal, you want to impose another on him against his will. You are acting like this is your home—not "our" home. You are acting like what *you* want is important, and what he wants is only an impediment to you. You are telling him that his home is not his safe, peaceful haven.

CALLER: Oh, my gosh, I didn't really see that. Yes, I guess that's right—that's how he probably sees it.

DR. LAURA: And what do you think you'll ultimately get in return for that attitude?

CALLER: Got it.

Some of the more cynical types might say that this caller is oppressed by her husband's whim, but those "types" are not going to ever be happily married to someone happily married to them. There is a necessary give-and-take, a benevolent cooperation between spouses that results in each feeling and believing that they deeply matter to the other. That, of course, is more important than simply getting another pet or getting one's own way by overpowering the other.

Whether it's whims or tastes should not be the important issue—being fair and loving is. Think about the typical home; it is largely decorated by the choices and tastes and whims of the woman of the house. Real estate agents have told me that they really need to sell a house to the wife because it is generally her reaction that motivates the man. Husbands defer to their wives because they love them and want to please them, and because (girls, we have to be honest) we make life hell for them when they don't. Since men live for our approval and acceptance, they are too easy to manipulate inappropriately, insensitively, inhumanely, and unlovingly.

One female caller to my radio program provided a great example of such manipulation. It seems that her husband has always hated chicken, even from as far back as when he was just her boyfriend. He probably ate some bad chicken when he was younger, or became ill after a meal and assumed it was the chicken. Just about everybody has had some experience like that, and we just don't want to ever eat that food again! No big deal.

But it was a big deal to my caller. She had been cooking him chicken cutlets and such, and telling him that it was turkey, since he had no problem eating that. She called to ask me if she should tell him the truth.

DR. LAURA: Why would you do that?

CALLER: Because, well, two reasons, actually. I wanted to prove to him that he didn't hate chicken. And it's just too annoying to cook chicken and turkey when I can just cook chicken.

DR. LAURA: You never cook something separate for the children or friends or relatives?

CALLER: Yeah, I do . . . but that's different.

DR. LAURA: How?

CALLER: (avoiding the question) Well, anyway, I want to know if I should tell him that he's been eating chicken, and see, it's fine!

DR. LAURA: No, absolutely not. And I think you should be cooking him turkey—as he asked you and as you said you were. If you want to offer him a bite of your chicken to see if he's still sensitive to it, that would show real caring and respect.

If you tell him what you've been doing to him to (a) risk getting him sick and (b) getting him into a "gotcha" moment, he's going to feel betrayed, humiliated, and definitely disrespected.

While the "chicken caper" may seem like a small thing, it isn't. When one adds up all those little moments when a husband is proven wrong or overpowered, we end up with one unhappy man. Then I get the calls about his not coming home on time, not being romantic, not listening, not—well, you get the idea. And, no wonder, because when you put garbage in, you get garbage out.

Steve, a listener, responded to my on-air discussions on how a wife should treat her husband. This is not, he remarked, a subject one hears much about.

"In today's world it is assumed that men are pigs and women suffer. With all my efforts (car and lawn maintenance, tending to children, working full time) I am not appreciated. It's never enough. It is common for the woman to expect the man to do uncomfortable things to help the relationship. I do not particularly like buying flowers or presents, shopping, having chitchat, dressing nice . . . but I do it because it is important to my wife.

However, for some reason, if there is anything at all I would like, but my wife feels 'uncomfortable,' it is out of the question! She feels that as a woman she should not have to do anything uncomfortable. Double standard!

The other double standard is that it is okay for women to criticize, put down, become grouchy, but if I'm feeling similarly, it is called verbal abuse. When I asked why that is so, I am told it's because I'm a man and they abuse, women don't!

I've got news for everyone: Men are hurt just as much by

abuse, or hurtful words, as women. Any form of coercion to get a man to do what you want is not only unproductive, it is damaging. Just because I am married does not make me a slave. Men are human beings."

Steve's final sentiment, about being a "human being" and not a "slave," reflected a common grievance from the men who wrote to me about this subject. Most women think that their husbands should have a sense of humor about how "difficult" women can be, with their hormonal cycles, emotionality, (hyper)sensitivity, changeable minds, and so forth. Well, some men do, some men don't.

The men who do have a sense of humor about the mercurial and mysterious nature of women are husbands who get respect, appreciation, gratitude, and compassion; they get love returned in a way that's meaningful to them.

The men who don't share that sense of humor are the men whose wives feel that doing the laundry, cooking dinner, or taking care of the kids is adequate compensation for their husbands' work. While these things may be appreciated, by and large, they're things she'd be doing even if she were not married. Those are not acts, specifically and personally, directed to "her man." And it is definitely those personal acts that make the difference to a husband who yearns to be treated like "a man," and like "her man."

The destructive anti-male subtext of the modern feminist agenda is to blame for some of this because those folks argue that catering to or deferring to a husband is slave-like submission to the male. In fact, after the Southern Baptist Council published a statement on "submission," the media went crazy, railing against their so-called backward, oppressive notions about women.

The Reverend Shane Cornutt, from Alabama, was one of many in and out of the clergy who wrote me to clarify this issue:

"Over the past couple of weeks I have noticed that some of your lady callers have had questions on a wife's submission to her husband and how it deals with their Christian faith when faced with a moral problem.

Nowhere in the Bible is a woman told to blindly submit to the will of her husband. In fact, the first act of submission is on the husband's *part! The husband is to submit himself to Christ and the will of God. When he does this he is not setting himself up as master, but rather as servant of the Lord. Only then is the wife to submit to the will of her husband—because the will of her husband will be obedience to the Lord. So the wife is not submitting to the husband, but to God.*

As soon as the husband steps outside this and acts contrary to scripture, the woman is under no moral obligation whatsoever *to her husband to transgress the moral law! Women are not, and were never meant to be, set up as servants to men in the kingdom of God.*

A man is supposed to love his wife as Christ loves the church. That means that a husband is required to love, care for, nurture, protect, comfort, and even be willing to die for his wife. That is love."

The reverend ended his letter with an admonition to men, suggesting that if any man is upset because he feels his wife is not in "proper submission" to him, the problem is with the man!

Whether or not a wife is Christian, or religious at all for that matter, the issue of respect is too often confused with a fearful notion of blind submission, and that becomes a stumbling block to the simple act of *giving*.

Rather than see this, though, for many women, it's easier to wallow in that self-pity mode. Lisa, a listener, is a married mother of two children, one six years old and the other nine months. She's new to being a stay-at-home mom and has adjusted her life to include an at-home business. When she and her husband did not have children and both worked full-time, they were more like equal partners in making a mess all week and then feverishly cleaning up on Friday night to afford themselves leisure time over the weekend. Now that she is at home, he leaves the household issues totally to her—and she's angry about it.

> "I just get so frustrated that I find myself complaining loudly throughout the day as I pick up the mess left the night before. I really resent at times that my role as companion has changed to housekeeper, maid, and nanny. Listening to the Dr. Laura show helps balance my views. I really need the reminders sometimes that Joel, my husband, works very hard to support us at a job that he does not enjoy, and that is physically taxing.
>
> I really respect that he rarely if ever takes a sick day. I know he works hard and I think he would love to be able to stay home as I do with our children. I try not to let the negative thinking overwhelm me. I still get mad when I have to pick up glasses from the living room or clothing from the floor, but I married a wonderful man who has never intentionally done anything to make my life more difficult. I don't have it so bad after all.
>
> It helps to reflect on reasons I married Joel in the first place. I married a man I truly respect, knowing that he is faithful and loving."

I get many calls from at-home wives who complain that when their husbands get home, they, the husbands, do not do various household chores. I generally challenge the women in return, asking, "Do you go to his work and make some of his calls, go to some of his meetings, help with filing or other clerical necessities?" Of course, the answer is, "Well, no . . . but." The point is not that the husband should be able to treat his wife like his personal maid, butler, or valet. The point is that in a division-of-labor situation, each has responsibilities, which, all totaled up at the end of the day or week, combine to take care of a family and household.

As one listener, Joanne, pointed out, "The care and feeding of husbands is, bottom line, to walk a mile in their shoes." Joanne's story is quite dramatic and instructive. She and her husband have two children; one has severe learning disabilities and the second has slight mental retardation. Until about five years ago, Joanne was the children's primary caretaker because her husband worked long hours. She felt deep resentment that she was alone at home fighting the battles with and for her children and their disabilities as well as doing all the household chores.

"And, of course, I let him know that I resented his long hours, though now looking back, that was a selfish thing to do because he was the major breadwinner. And he also did maintain the outside chores, i.e., lawn care, fixing up the house, painting, etc."

Five years ago their lives changed dramatically. After a serious injury on the job, Joanne's husband was no longer able to work like he used to. The situation at home has completely reversed, and he now does the bulk of the household chores, including the outside chores he always has, such as lawn care, car care, etc. And according to Joanne:

"NOT ONCE does he complain! He makes sure the boys are taken care of. He is even teaching them how to drive. As I look back on how I acted toward my husband's long hours, I feel guilty. After all, he was supporting us so that I COULD stay home and raise OUR two wonderful sons. I realize that now. The boys needed me then and they need their father now. And because of all this wonderful time with Dad, they are turning

into wonderful, productive young adults. Because of my hus-
band's health problems, our sons do a whole lot around the
house to help their dad and me. They have learned a lot of
responsibility and see how important it is for a family unit to
come together during hard times as well as good times."

The issue of "roles" in a marriage and family is often a sensitive one. Stay-at-home moms as well as hardworking, primary-breadwinner men are not given much respect from our society-at-large. Feminist educators and activists keep trying to squeeze men and women into niches that may simply not be a good match for their innate qualities as individuals as well as their unique masculine and feminine drives.

It is more in the female nature to nest and nurture. It is more in the male nature to conquer and protect. Frankly, the more we ignore the true, inherent masculine and feminine qualities of people, the farther apart we pull them.

Most all of the women who call me who have reversed the traditional societal roles—that is, have a husband at home with the children—are troubled by the fact that they seem to have less regard for their husbands as "men." Likewise, they report a diminished sense of their own femininity, and suffer ferocious guilt over not being their children's primary caretaker. This does not mean that this situation is not workable, but it is a delicate balancing act and it requires husbands and wives to be creative in complementing and augmenting their partner's feminine and masculine needs.

Interestingly, a major study reported in April 2002 at an American Heart Association forum concluded, after following patterns of heart disease and death among nearly four thousand participants for ten years, that men and women who defy traditional societal roles may suffer more health consequences, such as heart disease, than those who adhere to traditional roles. According to an ABC News report:

"The investigators did not find that high amounts of job stress, characterized as having high demands with little autonomy, was associated with an increased risk of heart disease. However, they did find that women who were in positions of high authority with high job demands suffered higher rates of heart disease than other women, although their male counterparts did not. Similarly, men who dubbed themselves primarily as house-husbands—about 10 percent of the participants—had an 82 percent higher ten-year death rate than men who worked out-side the home."

The researchers took into account such factors as smoking, age, anxiety, stress, household responsibilities, blood pressure, weight, cholesterol levels, diabetes, and others.

While obviously the differences in individuals would make it wrong to limit or judge personal choices, I believe that ulti-mately the well-being of both men and women is maximized when acceptance, attention, and nurturance is given to what is innately different and special about men and women.

And, with respect to the Proper Care and Feeding of Husbands, we can take direction from folks like this listener:

"Although at thirty-one I am still unmarried, I've noticed that my father reacts much better to my mother when she needs him and acts like he's an important and integral part of her life."

Curtis, another listener, adds:

"All of us men have been told for years now that a woman 'needs' to be listened to. We're told not to try to solve the prob-lem or to advise her, just listen and be sympathetic to her needs. Most women don't understand why men haven't learned this by now. Here's why! What she doesn't seem to understand is I really do want to be her White Knight. I really do want to come

riding to her rescue. I really do want to sweep her off her feet and carry her away and live happily ever after."

The most poignant part of Curtis's letter followed. He talked about the never-ending job of listening without rescuing that he was supposed to do for his wife in order to be a sensitive husband. However, when she was finishing venting, and felt better having gotten whatever it was off her chest, the problem for her was gone, but the problem for him had just begun.

Because he's supposed to just be a listening board (like a girlfriend or shrink?) and not help solve, repair, or attack her enemies, he is quiet. Why? Because he's failed, in his eyes, to be a man, her man. He's worthless, impotent to help her, to stop her pain.

"I've been relegated to being the warm, soft, cuddly teddy bear on her bed, instead of the white knight in her bed. I don't feel like a man. My self-esteem is in the bottom of the well. I just want to be a man with the woman I love in my arms."

This is an important lesson that not too many women appear to be getting from their own mothers or because of the modeling of their childhood family life. Amber, a listener, wrote that about a year ago (and seven years into her marriage), she and her girlfriend decided to learn how to be better wives to their husbands.

"And to our shame, we really learned a lot. In essence, I've learned what you teach, preach, and nag about: that my mother's four dysfunctional marriages and our culture taught me to disrespect my husband and to take his love for granted. I freely and cruelly criticized him, privately and (shamefully) publicly. I tried to control everything, especially finances, because

I erroneously thought that he couldn't handle things as well as I could. I couldn't bear the thought of anything controlling ME, so I had to be the one in control."

After studying Scripture, reading, and listening to my program, Amber realized how destructive her attitudes toward her husband had been. She asked herself the following very important questions, which every wife should ask herself: If I really believe all the things I say/think/complain about him, why on earth are we married? If I love him so much, why do I act so unloving and disrespectful? What will make him continue to love me if I continue to act this way?

I have been using that latter question lately on my program to get women to pause and think about the destructive nature of their behavior toward their husbands. For example, recently a twenty-something female caller asked me whether it was fair or not to get her husband to shave off his beard. He didn't have one when they were dating, or at any time since they married some three years ago, but had grown one recently. Shamefully, she had already told him that she didn't find him as attractive with the beard.

I responded with sadness in my voice. "Tell me, how much more indignity could a husband experience at the hands of his wife than not being allowed to decide for himself whether or not to have facial hair?"

I further surprised her by calling her comment to him about not finding him as attractive with the beard *abusive*. It is sad how much abuse (criticism, nagging, blaming, yelling) women can heap on men without seeing it as hurtful and abusive, even as they themselves are so hypersensitive about any apparent (even unintended) slight or reaction of their men to them. Double standard, I say.

Wives do tend to be controlling—in ways we perhaps don't even recognize as such. Just before I went to bed last night, I turned on the television for a last-minute news update, and in going past channels to my usual news station, I paused at a sit-com. I don't know the characters or the plot, or even the name of the show, but I saw what appeared to be a father talking to his grown son in his son's fiancée's presence. The father said something like, "Son, you are a man and you can make any decision you believe in and feel is right . . . until you're married—then your wife will be making all your decisions for you."

While the laugh track did its thing, I immediately realized that the controlling of men by their wives is so taken for granted that a sitcom could use it as a source of humor with no one imagining it was a true slap against women.

Alexis, one of my listeners, struggled with this concept of controlling and changing a husband into a wife's perfect picture of a mate.

"I remember a perfect example of how I set myself up with high expectations. Before we were married, I was going to his house for dinner, and on the way I had this image playing in my mind that I'd get there and he'd come to the door and hug and kiss me and his house would be spotless and he'd have a big bouquet of roses for me and the table was set and the dinner was ready and soft music was playing, etc.

I get there, knock three times, and finally just open the door myself. He's lying on the couch watching sports, dishes are in the sink, no food, no flowers, no music, and he says with a smile, 'Hi, babe,' no different than any other time . . . and I was mad at him.

I realized I had set him up in my mind to be something I know he isn't. He's casual and unromantic. What you see is what you get. But he's moral, loving, and has a very strong religious faith. He stands up for what's right. He's funny and intelligent and he loves me for who I am, so shouldn't I love him for who he is?"

When you put it that way, what's a little bit of facial hair?

Instead of appreciating a man for his unique and manly qualities, too many wives constantly complain—to the husbands themselves and to friends, neighbors, family, and sometimes even to the children.

One caller recently asked me if she was wrong to "vent" her annoyance with her husband to her ten-year-old son. She said that her husband told her that she did that to recruit their son to her side in their issues and thereby undermine his bond with his own child. In her own defense, she said that she thought her son had a right to know what was going on— and, she admitted, she wanted his sympathy.

Not only is this disrespecting a husband and father in his own home by trying to make him look bad to his family, it is completely inappropriate and psychologically abusive to burden children with parental issues and force them to give up one parent for the sake of the other.

I suggested, and she was agreeable, that she apologize to her son for triangulating him into their skirmish, and that she apologize to her husband for such dirty tricks.

Another listener wrote in to confess that she used to be hypercritical of her husband. Now she's learned that he may not do things the way she would, but that he gets the job done.

> "And in the end, it doesn't much matter that they eat PBJ sandwiches for breakfast, lunch, and dinner for a day or that one tooth brushing gets overlooked or whatever little thing that used to set me off!
>
> What matters is that our sons have learned that their daddy is an awesome, competent, and loving caretaker. More important, I have learned that I set an example for my sons of how a wife should act. Would I want my sons to marry someone who treats them the way I used to treat my own husband? NO!"

Showing respect for a husband in his own home not only sends him a message that he's loved and appreciated, it sets the game plan for the next generation's marriages. How much more important could it get?

Becky, another listener, wrote that her mother warned her early on not to come to her with complaints, criticisms, and gripes about her husband.

> *"My mother, I believe, had the best advice; in fact, I follow it to this day as a married woman. The general idea behind her words was simple: If you want me to love and respect the man you date and eventually marry, don't come to me with complaints about all his faults and weaknesses. You may forgive his words and actions easily; I, however, am your mother, and I don't like to see you hurt. It will take more for me to accept his apologies than it will for you."*

Becky admitted that at times this great advice wasn't easy to follow. There were days when she just wanted to vent to someone all of her frustrations on some point. However, when that happened, she would stop and think about what her mother had told her and, as she said, realize that "no emotional outlet is worth damaging my husband's reputation."

In opening this chapter, I quoted one of my listeners, Wendi, who said, "It is easy for a woman to love; that is the way that God made her. It is more difficult for her to show respect." This is a sad but important truth. Wendi's letter continued: "Respect means treating someone in an edifying manner, never denigrating or attacking."

She acknowledges in her letter that when she and her husband married sixteen years ago, they did not know how to communicate with fairness and respect. Although like all newlyweds, they promised to be friends, they fell into that familiar trap of too much "familiarity," treating each other worse than they would treat strangers or acquaintances. They would say they loved each other, but their actions and words would appear to disprove that sentiment.

Finally turning to a more religious, spiritual course, Wendi chose to see her husband as a gift from God, thereby someone deserving of respect.

> *"Even when times were difficult, I tried to look beyond what was happening and see him as God saw him. When I began to show my husband respect, he did not reciprocate—at first. And it was difficult to do what God required when no progress was obvious.*
>
> *But God was working on his heart, healing old hurts and wounds that I had created, allowing him to know that he could trust me to stick to our vows. The change in my husband from that time forward has been dramatic. We are a team. We respect one another. We try to place the other's needs above our own, in full confidence that our own needs will be met by our spouse.*
>
> *Learning to see beyond and reflecting God's love to my husband made all the difference. Making the decision to respect the man God had given me made all the difference."*

What does it actually mean, in concrete terms, to treat one's husband with respect? To start with, a man likes and needs to be treated like he is "the man." That seems to be difficult for a lot of women to do, partly because they have been brought up with notions of "unisexuality," the sadly mistaken and destructive belief that men and women have no differences—and whatever men want or do that women don't appreciate is stupid, wasteful, and self-indulgent. Well, the fact is, men and women *are* different physically, psychologically, motivationally, and temperamentally. Anyone who has had exposure to babies and children can tell you that boys and girls respond differently to the world right from the start. Give both a doll and the girl will cuddle it, while the boy will more likely use it as a projectile or weapon. Give them two dolls and the girl will have the dolls talking to each other, while the boy will have them engage in combat.

On my radio program, I have related an experience that vividly points out the subtleties of masculinity and femininity in parenting. I was at a swimming pool, watching a mom and dad play with their infant child. First, the mother, holding the baby against her chest, cooed to the baby and playfully swooped him up and down. After a while, she passed the baby to Dad, who immediately turned the baby's face outward, and swooshed the baby forward and up into the air. My conclusion? Mom equals protection and nurturance. Dad equals autonomy and adventure. It is that perfect balance that helps produce a functional, secure human being.

When a wife treats her man like he's one of her children, when she puts him down or thwarts his need for autonomy, adventure, risk, competition, challenge, and conquest, she ends up with a sullen, uncooperative, unloving, hostile lump.

Tammy, a listener, learned to follow her father's advice, cited earlier: ("You are marrying a man. Always treat him like one and he will always act like one.")

"I have noticed that in every area of our marriage, work, home, family, children, career, David excels when I treat him like a man.

I mean by this that I do not demand he do things. I ask. I suggest options for his problems and then let him pick one. I never differ with him in front of the children. I do not deal with his family in an unpleasant situation—I let him deal with his family.

I never do anything to embarrass him or make him feel less manly in front of his family, coworkers, children, neighbors, or friends.

> *Let me tell you what this gets me. It gets me a man who is
> so comfortable with his masculinity that he can focus on being
> tender and loving and giving to me constantly because he is
> never concerned about protecting his ego or proving he is the
> 'man of the house.' I do that for him."*

I believe most women don't appreciate how much they
are responsible for the tone of the home and the entire family. This statement is not about placing fault or blame, it is
about acknowledging the incredible power women have in
impacting those around them. Both children and husbands are
inexorably dependent upon the approval, appreciation, and
acceptance of Mom. Without that, they are desolate—and
they behave badly.

CJ, another listener, wrote to me that she was about five
years and four kids into her marriage when resentment hit.
She was tired of her schedule—the cleaning, the kids, the dinner, the shopping, the everything! She even began to lose her
sense of being in love with her husband.

And so she decided to develop a sense of humor. She
started to cut back on "chores" and focus instead on paying
more direct attention to her husband. This is, of course, the
complete opposite of what pop psych and women's magazines
suggest. These sources generally recommend that when a
woman is "fed up" with her life, it's time for spas, solo vacations, more girlfriend time, plastic surgery, affairs, or divorce.
This is all in the search for "getting one's own needs met."

But CJ decided to turn that energy into affection and attention toward her husband. How did that get her needs met?

> *"I started to ignore the house and pay more attention to him.
> Instead of just telling him I loved him, I told him I adored
> him. I made those little calls during the day just to remind him.
> When he came home tired, I started to indulge him, and not
> resent him. When in mixed company, I always went out of my*

way to compliment what he's done for me or the kids. I always brag about what a great dad he is.

I realized that I CHOSE this life, so I made myself appreciate ALL I had, and pretty soon I believed it!

You may call it stroking his ego, but it paid off. The more attention I paid, the more I got. He was not as interested in a perfect house as he was in having an adoring wife. I became her and thus fell back in love with my husband and life.

In return, he showed his love for me. I learned that MY MOOD set the mood for the house."

And since when did sincere stroking of a husband's ego fall into disrepute? Probably when the feminists decided that caring for a man was tantamount to a betrayal of the sisterhood. Too many women lost too many wonderful opportunities to have a happy and fulfilling life by buying into the destructive notion that a woman becomes more if she sees and treats men as less.

On my radio program, I hear from too many women who believe that they are somehow entitled to have all their needs, wants, desires, and whims met by life in general, and by their men in particular, no matter what choices they've made and no matter how poorly they treat their men.

The two major categories for these complaints are domestic and emotional. Kelly, a listener, wrote in to respond to a caller on my program who went on and on about her husband not meeting her "emotional needs." Kelly acknowledged that she, too, had been caught in that trap during most of her thirties, but she now reflects on that time as a waste of a decade because she spent countless hours husband-bashing because he wasn't meeting her emotional needs.

"This is such a pitfall of pop psychology and really has more to do with the baggage that one brings into the marriage than the truth of the matter: Marriage is a lot of hard work. And when

*you are raising kids together, with Mom staying at home, it cre-
ates an awful burden on the husband to do what he has to do
in order to financially support the entire family on one income. I
never fully gave my husband credit for, as you say, Dr. Laura,
'slaying the dragon' all those years while I stayed at home—all
the while complaining that he wasn't meeting my emotional
needs."*

Kelly's perspective changed when it was discovered she had
a brain tumor. Her so-called "emotionless" husband sat by her
bedside in the hospital for nearly three days straight, became
both father and mother to their children for her nearly three
months of treatment and recovery, and somehow managed to
still get himself up and off to work every day to provide for
the family. She became a firm believer that God will do what
He must in order to get your attention at times—and she
learned the lesson.

She developed a new appreciation and love for her husband. She learned to respect his masculine approach to life,
family, challenges, and problems.

Men rescue, repair, provide, protect. Men don't sit, stew, and
rehash. Men are active and proactive. They do that out of love,
duty, responsibility, and character. That needs to be respected
and appreciated if a woman is to have a happy life married to a
good man. A good man is just that—a man. A good man is not
a best girlfriend.

Stephanie, a listener, wrote:

*"I am so excited that someone is finally tackling this issue. I
did not realize how destructive I was to my marriage until I
heard you say a few times that for the spouse who chooses to
stay home with the children, it is their responsibility to cook,
clean, do laundry, and perform all those mundane tasks that
keep a home running so that the other spouse can go out and
earn the money that helps this family succeed."*

Stephanie had been married for almost two years and had a nine-month-old baby boy—a surprise that took her out of the workplace and into the home. It only took her a few months to become resentful at what she interpreted as her husband's "freedom" compared with her feeling chained down at home. She never spoke about her feelings; instead she took them out on her husband by "not being in the mood for sex."

She, like many women, found it difficult to give up the work world since she had defined herself by the position she held with her company. She missed the daily kudos and the calls she would receive asking for her opinions. She missed the excitement of travel and the constant challenges and new input.

At some point, though, she had an epiphany: "I am fortunate beyond what I deserve." She describes a family that has most breakfasts, lunches, and dinners together, a husband who is the most well-balanced executive she knows.

> *"Nothing is more important than our marriage and our son. I appreciate my husband more than he will ever know. Since I had this epiphany, our marriage has changed. It's romantic, loving, respectful, and intimate.*
>
> *Our greatest hope for our son and future children is to learn what it means to be a family and to make sacrifices for the betterment of others and give of themselves by seeing their family growing stronger every day. My husband and I will be giddy when our son and his future wife provide our grandchildren the same loving and nurturing environment.*
>
> *Maybe family values will become popular again, and this craze of women destroying their families in the quest to have it all will become passé."*

Perhaps the feminist notions about women having power if they do it all has obstructed too many women's ability to realize that in real life we all make choices, and that the true joy and meaning of life is not in how many things we have or do, but in the sacrifice and commitment we make to others within the context of the choices we've made. The Tenth Commandment, about coveting, reminds us that none of us can have everything there is to have nor everything we want. Without enjoying and appreciating our gifts and blessings, we create hell on earth for ourselves and for those who love us.

Jennifer called my show complaining about her emergency-room-physician husband.

JENNIFER: I am my kids' mom. I have a five-year-old and a three-year-old—both boys. My husband voluntarily takes extra hours at work to make up for a pay cut that happened this year. We don't need the extra money. And I need him at home.

DR. LAURA: To do what?

JENNIFER: To be a father.

DR. LAURA: What hours is he working?

JENNIFER: Twelve-hour days, four days a week, and he's sometimes on call.

DR. LAURA: You were aware when you were sold in marriage from some Eastern Bloc country that you were marrying a physician, right? Perhaps you didn't understand the life of a physician's wife—which means assuming much more personal responsibility for home and kids.

JENNIFER: I know he measures everything by his wallet, whether he's successful or not, and he wants to try to retire early. I understand all that. Is it wrong for me to go about what I'd like to do while he's at work—go see my sister and do the things that I want to do? And would it be unsupportive if I'm not home when he gets home?

DR. LAURA: Yeah, that would be unsupportive. Go see

your sister, but get home in time to have a hot dinner there. Because that's your part of taking care of the family—and he's doing his part.

JENNIFER: But we don't need that extra money.

DR. LAURA: Because he's trying to make up for the money he lost when he got a pay cut, somehow he's a greedy, avaricious type?

JENNIFER: I don't think that.

DR. LAURA: That's what I got out of what you said. You have a lot of hostility. You didn't marry a nine-to-five type. You married someone with a profession—a calling. He works in urgent care. That requires a special mentality, dealing with life-and-death crises, allaying people's anxiety, fixing body parts.

You need to be supportive that you have a man who is trying very hard to take care of his family and get them in a position where there is no financial problem. The hours he works sound very much like those of a fireman. You have to do your part—he has his.

You can take the two kids and go to a movie in the middle of the day while he's cleaning up blood and pus. I don't really want to hear your grumbling about the hours he's working because they are not glamorous hours—they're pretty nauseating, considering most of the things he has to do.

You have a tremendous amount of freedom to do whatever you want. When both kids are in school, you can use those hours in constructive ways. I think you ought to be more grateful to him that he's working his buns off to keep all of you really solvent and independent *and* that he's doing something that is just a blessing to the earth: helping all kinds of people who are sick and dying in pain. I think you need to show more respect for what he's doing for them and for you and your family.

So go do what you want to do all day, and make sure a hot dinner is there, served with a smile and a hug, when he gets home. Because the more you create an atmosphere that shows you appreciate what he does when he's out there, the more he's going to want to be home.

Finally, one husband sent me a copy of a letter to his wife he'd been up until two o'clock in the morning writing. He considered it a significant coincidence considering the announced subject of this book.

Evidently, he'd been trying to communicate to his wife his feelings and thoughts about the texture and direction of their marriage. Her quickie solution to their problems, it seems, was to suggest a two-week visit to Disneyland. He did not feel that trip would be the miracle to improve the marriage.

This man's letter, I believe, represents a universal truth that has been denied and largely lost by a culture hell-bent on measuring human value through power and money. That truth is that the family needs a woman and a man, a husband and a wife, a father and a mother, much more than it needs the equal power of two career-oriented people.

He writes to his wife:

"I'm learning more as the years go by that you are a career-oriented person who doesn't have a clue or understand the essence of what it means to be a wife and mother. Call me traditional if you like, but I firmly believe that mothers need to spend more time at home, perhaps 100 percent of their time at home, to nurture a family and develop a home.

Far too often, there are too many things that get overlooked by you as a wife and mother as it pertains to this family. Our kids lack focus, training, and discipline. They have no routine and there's no order about anything that they do. Mothers, in my opinion, are nurturers and teachers who ought to spend as much time with their kids to teach them things, skills that they will use to cope with life. To put it bluntly, you haven't been a mother. Our kids have been left too often to cope and figure out things for themselves.

When it comes to being a wife, you put no effort. And I think you don't love me anymore. Making love is not high on your agenda of things to do, and showing any intimate interest in me isn't either.

I'm feeling less and less interested in you and less and less motivated to keep this family together. I'm feeling like you are married to your job and that you are more committed to it than to us as a wife and mother.

I'm not claiming that I'm the perfect husband and father. You and I both work too many hours, but I believe you underestimate the importance of the mother in a family. Mothers and fathers play different roles in a family. I've never discouraged you from pursuing a Ph.D., but I don't think it's high on the list of priorities of what I think is best for us as a family right now.

I want to love you, be with you, and support you, but I must confess that I'm feeling like we are losing each other and our kids. I don't know what the complete answer is, but I believe it has to start with us spending more time at home to grow, develop, and nurture our family and our relationship."

The notion of "fixed roles" is inflammatory and controversial. It shouldn't be so. I've said many times on my program that women have become denigrated by that part of the feminist movement that dismisses marriage, child rearing, and home-making as insignificant and insulting to women. Promiscuity, shacking up, abortions, illegitimacy, rush-hour traffic, and office politics are a boon to women?

I am a working wife and mother, and I appreciate the

opportunity to use my skills and talents to be creative in something I believe is meaningful. Nonetheless, I consider my first and foremost responsibility to be "my kids' mom." I work my career around my family—and not the other way around. My deepest satisfactions in life come from a tall, skinny but muscular teenage boy saying "I love you" (even in front of his buddies) and a husband of almost two decades who still calls me "beautiful."

As long as women disrespect what they have to offer as wives and mothers, they will continue to disrespect their men who serve as husbands and fathers. No one benefits. No one is happy.

Chapter 8

GUY TIME

"A woman would do well to understand that an honest, faithful husband who goes on a three-week hunting trip is not telling her he doesn't love her. He just wants to kill something. Nothing more complicated than that."

JOSH

Sabino called my program to ask me who was right, him or his wife. The situation causing the problem concerned a weekend trip to Seattle he and his wife had planned as a little get-away time. Then Sabino happened to mention the trip to his buddy, a married neighbor with kids just down the block. His buddy thought this weekend jaunt was a great idea and offered up himself and his family to Sabino as company on the trip. Sabino didn't want to disappoint or hurt his buddy, so he said, "Fine."

Well, it wasn't fine with Sabino's wife, who had been looking forward to quiet, intimate family and personal time.

Sabino wanted my opinion. Was he kidding?

This is not an example of legitimate, healthy, even necessary "guy time." This is an example of insensitive (and stupid) behavior that demonstrates a profound lack of maturity and responsibility within a marriage. When a fellow is more concerned about disappointing his buddy than his woman, he has virtually cut up his "manhood" card and retrieved his adolescent-male card from what should have been his past.

It seemed that Sabino had his definitions backward. He thought being a man meant standing up to his woman and standing with his buddies. But a real man can stand up to his buddies and stand with his woman *and* believe that this highlights and intensifies his masculinity rather than diminishes it—because he is not about image, he is about substance, and that substance consists of respect and commitment.

Now, on the other side, too many women are outright hostile and pouty about a man's need for guy time. I can't tell you how many calls I get from wives who are deeply resentful that their men want to take some time for themselves and maybe spend it with their male friends. Usually what they end up doing is playing some sport (like golf, basketball, or baseball), watching some sport (that generally includes nachos and beer), going on a trip (oftentimes to fish, hunt, or rock-climb), or something as tame as playing poker (more nachos and beer).

Where does that wifely resentment come from? While the arguments given by these wives to explain why they object to their husbands' guy time vary tremendously, the core issue seems to be insecurity. This insecurity could be about a fear that their husbands might not really enjoy their company, or that they don't know how to be alone without feeling bad about themselves, or that they are envious of their husbands' ability to have hobbies and friends, or that they worry that their husbands, while out of their influence and control, might not evaluate their relationship and family situation as desirable. Also, many women have the notion that everything in the marriage and family must have them at the center to be valid and acceptable.

Recently, a woman called about her military husband, who is in a band. She was upset because he'd agreed to a gig on Valentine's Day, without checking with her first, and she called to ask if it was reasonable for her to be upset.

I took her back to the time before her marriage and asked whether her husband had been involved in music then. She reported that he's always been into music, and joined up with his current band while they were engaged.

"Honey," I said, "you've got to learn to accept what kind of animal you brought home. You can't knowingly bring home an elephant and then expect it to curl up in your lap and purr."

This is a big problem for many women. They believe that after marriage, the husband will become completely domesticated and she will be the master; the whip will be *her desires and feelings*. Men do put up with that to a certain point . . . and then they don't.

I suggested to her that she rent a room at the hotel at which her husband's band was playing on Valentine's Day, go to his gig, and then take him upstairs to wine, candles, and a sexy negligee. I reminded her that her main dilemma was the acceptance of her own choices.

One listener wrote in about this very dilemma. However, she finally figured out what kind of animal she had brought home and stopped trying to threaten it into being the kind of animal she thought she wanted. It paid off. She wrote:

"Early in our marriage I discovered myself resenting my husband for all the Saturday and Sunday afternoons he spent playing golf. It became a constant source of tension between us until it finally dawned on me that he was not playing any more than he had during the two and a half years we were dating; I simply hadn't noticed it as much before we were living together.

I told him that I would stop badgering him because, after

all, doing what he enjoyed made him a happier person and a more content husband.

He now asks if I mind before he sets up a golf outing, plays less often overall, and pays more attention to me when he's not playing—all because he appreciates the change in my attitude."

This wife was smart. She thought about the two candidates in the election: candidate #1, being angry all the time and ruining her own life as well as her and her husband's life together with her constant resentment, or candidate #2, accepting the kind of animal she brought home and reframing his traits in the positive. She ultimately voted for #2, and it changed everything. Why? Because he no longer saw his wife as somebody chipping away at who he was and what he did. He saw a wife appreciating the man he actually was—and that made him want to be more of that for her.

It's worth repeating that men yearn for, first, their mothers' acceptance, approval, and appreciation, and then their wives', and when they get those three A's, they'll do just about anything to please their wives.

Brian, another listener, wrote about what he saw universally—not just in his own home—as a double standard regarding time spent apart.

"When the issue of friends comes up, it's usually that she's allowed to go out almost at will, with little regard for what I might have planned. But if I were to want to spend some time with friends, it's usually a fight waiting to happen! She says she feels like I should trust her and allow her freedom. However, when the shoe is on the other foot, and I want to spend some time with friends, according to her it's that I don't love her or want to spend time with her. Even if she's invited!

I feel this is a form of manipulation: wanting to have things her way and not wanting to give me the same. Basically, it's she that matters."

And that is the message that too many husbands get. They begin to realize that their feelings, needs, and desires are really not that relevant to their wives, or are perceived only as annoyances and impediments to the wives' more important motivations.

This is not the way to keep a man happy—or to keep a man at all. As one listener, Jim, wrote:

> *"Wives want romance, hugs, kisses, and surprises. They would get more of these things if they hadn't just told hubby he was stupid or that a night out with the guys was tantamount to abandonment . . . or that four hours out of 168 to myself is being overly selfish or self-indulgent."*

When men call my radio program to complain about not getting support from their wives for guy time, they let me know the magnitude of their frustration by listing all the things they do for their wives and families, as a way of defending themselves against charges of being selfish, uninvolved, or negligent. These men are involved in family activities and outings, and work around the house on the weekends and evenings when needed. They cook, do dishes, fix the cars, repair the house, mow the lawn, trim the hedges, go to kids' sporting events and school functions, drive kids to and from their activities and school, stop off at the market on the way home, even "baby-sit" the kids when the wife wants to go off to shop, eat lunch out with her mother or girlfriends, or go to aerobics.

Not only do these men suffer criticisms for the precise way they do or don't do all of the above, they are begrudged the guy time they need in order to blow off steam, work off nervous tension and energy, reconnect with their animal-level masculinity, briefly relieve themselves of the stress of responsibilities, or just have some fun to keep sane and happy.

Many times wives will undermine these efforts by scheduling family visits or doctor appointments, or by complaining about being ill or so exhausted from their week, or so emotionally distraught from some interpersonal problem, that they need their husbands home.

I believe that women basically take men for granted and want to mold them into an image they have in their own minds of what a husband—their husband—should be. This takes me back to the metaphor of the "animal you chose to bring home." Women will often be attracted to the athletic, musical, accomplished, involved, outgoing kind of guy for not necessarily the right reasons. If they are attracted to these active men because they admire those qualities, and expect to support those qualities, that's good. But if they are attracted to these active men because they are like groupies who bask in the men's glow, who think they can acquire a value and identity by association with "greatness," that's bad. The former means that they are a good match. The latter means that they are a match that will light the fuse for a big explosion.

Another listener who married a musician shares this story about her transformation from the "latter" to the "former."

"First, my husband and I were married after just four months of serious dating after knowing each other for one year. He was really into playing music, but I didn't figure that it would still take the number one position in his life. I thought that I would. For many years I would be very angry when he would leave for his practices and performances. It took me about seven years to realize that I could not change him and his desire for his music. He told me once that it was his escape.

After many angry nights, fights, and threatening to leave, I have accepted the fact that he does need this escape. Now I have learned to use the time that he is gone to have some private time of my own. Now it seems that if his practice is canceled and he is home, I am a little bummed because I don't have that special quiet time of my own.

We've been married for nine years, and after listening to your show, I have put much of my silly things aside and have realized that my husband is a truly good and loving husband . . . just not in every way that I 'expected' him to be."

Her letter reveals a very important point, which is that many women expect their husbands to always bend to their, the wives', whim and will, but that their lives are like a letter, completely dependent upon someone else's writing. In other words, marriage should not mean that either partner takes complete responsibility for the other's well-being, activities, or state of mind. Marriage does mean we share—but it also means we support the individuality necessary for mental and emotional health, and for the ultimate well-being of the relationship.

Without this healthy balance, a marriage can decay or dissolve. Tansie, a listener, reveals that she learned this the hard way:

"I learned that husbands need to have interests outside of me! Whenever my now-ex-husband would visit his brothers or sisters or friends without me (which he only did for a few hours once per month or so), I would complain and act like a spoiled brat for days! Why didn't he want to spend every waking moment with me? Obviously, he didn't love me!

After a very painful divorce and lots of therapy, I have learned that husbands with friends and outside interests are happier. It adds to their happy relationship with you when you gracefully support their relationships with others and not behave like a spoiled brat who wants to control their lives."

Tansie now has a new "sweetheart," who loves to spend a few hours a week with friends and is always very excited to call her afterward to share how much fun he had. Tansie has cultivated hobbies and friends of her own now and is not depending on her man to be her *everything*.

Frankly, in order for either party in a marriage—as well as the children—to stay balanced and centered, a reasonable amount of quiet time, alone time, is necessary. Now, the desire and need for this time may fluctuate depending on what's going on in your life, but in most cases it's a good antidote to stress, and stress is a by-product even of everyday obligations, tasks, and responsibilities. Think of stress as a kind of static electricity on the brain and soul that has to be gotten rid of with either quiet contemplation or a complete change in activity. Don't begrudge yourself or your partner this necessary outlet, without which one's life and one's marriage can become an overfilled pressure cooker.

I believe that it is a responsibility of both spouses to refresh themselves so that they can give their best to their relationship and their family.

Sometimes the issue of schedules can become a good-intentioned bargaining chip! Keith, one of my listeners, writes:

> *"My wife has interests independent from me. In other words, she has friends and work and isn't totally dependent upon me for her happiness. While we are a team and work together on issues and do most things together, we also can enjoy some time on our own.*
>
> *The flip side is that my wife allows me some independence to play golf once in a while, to watch sports, etc.—in other words, lets me have some life on my own. She has let me bargain with her so that I can watch football on Sundays if I do the laundry. Talk about a win-win!*
>
> *I am not advocating total independence for each partner. But I believe one of the major reasons for our success is that in moderation we are able to pursue our own interests, and in comparison with other wives that I have observed, mine doesn't need*

*me to provide for her entertainment twenty-four hours a day.
Having other interests makes both of us more interesting to
each other."*

It didn't escape me that Keith used the words "allows" and
"lets me" when referring to his own opportunities for downtime or guy time. I don't believe these references necessarily
suggest that he is hen-pecked, I think they point out a universal truth that I have mentioned numerous times in this book:
that men are raised by women as children and are embraced
by women as adults and look to women for those three A's.
This gives women tremendous power over men, power that
ought not be abused or overused; it is just too easy for a grown
man to turn into a rebellious child.

Women generally have tremendous opportunity to "hang
with their own kind." Wives should not begrudge their men
the necessity to do the same. Men need some space away from
femininity and domesticity in order to reassert an important
yet societally denigrated reality: Basic, fundamental, animal
masculinity needs to be respected. When men get their time
away, they come back to us better men.

Allison, a listener, has come to peace with this reality:

*"My husband and I have what we consider to be a very happy
marriage. Besides not trying to change each other, I have no
problem letting him have his 'guy time' with his buddies.
Mostly they get together in our garage (pool table, fridge) for
cards on Saturday nights—but not every week. They usually
don't start until after our kids are in bed, so there is no extra
burden on me.*

*He works hard all week and I believe he deserves some time
just to be a guy and do guy things. I usually use that time to
enjoy having control of the TV remote, work on the computer, or
do something just for me.*

He also gives me my time—it's not one-way.

Most of his friends' wives don't feel the same as I do, and they see the get-togethers as a bone of contention.

I think having that time makes him a more relaxed husband."

Allison is a smart woman and a smart wife.

Now you know how to be a smart—and happier—wife, too.

BOOKS BY DR. LAURA SCHLESSINGER

IN PRAISE OF STAY-AT-HOME MOMS

ISBN 978-0-06-169030-3 (pb) • ISBN 978-0-06-171197-8 (uab CD)

Dr. Laura celebrates a group of important yet overlooked women—stay-at-home moms—and offers them words of inspiration and wisdom.

STOP WHINING, START LIVING

ISBN 978-0-06-083834-8 (pb) • ISBN 978-0-06-145637-4 (uab CD)

Staying stuck in whining mode can become a life-long problem. Dr. Laura steps in to help folks conquer the temptation to retreat from living life to the fullest.

THE PROPER CARE & FEEDING OF MARRIAGE

ISBN 978-0-06-114284-0 (hc) • ISBN 978-0-06-114282-6 (pb)
ISBN 978-0-06-123399-9 (uab CD) • ISBN 978-0-06-122711-0 (CD)

In this *New York Times* bestseller, Dr. Laura encourages married partners to take a hard look at themselves and each other.

BAD CHILDHOOD—GOOD LIFE
How to Blossom and Thrive in Spite of an Unhappy Childhood

ISBN 978-0-06-057786-5 (hc) • ISBN 978-0-06-057787-2 (pb)
ISBN 978-0-06-085288-7 (CD)

Dr. Laura shows men and women that they can have a Good Life no matter how bad their childhood.

THE PROPER CARE & FEEDING OF HUSBANDS

ISBN 978-0-06-052061-8 (hc) • ISBN 978-0-06-052062-5 (pb)
ISBN 978-0-06-056675-3 (CD)

Dr. Laura reminds women that to take proper care of their husbands is to ensure themselves the happiness and satisfaction they yearn for.

WOMAN POWER
Transform Your Man, Your Marriage, Your Life

ISBN 978-0-06-083363-3 (pb)

Discover the special power women have to transform their husbands, their marriages, and their lives.

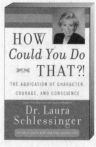